American Book Company's

MASTERING THE
GEORGIA 4TH GRADE CRCT
IN
ENGLISH LANGUAGE ARTS

Sara Hinton

Lisa M. Cocca

Project Coordinator: Zuzana Urbanek
Executive Editor: Dr. Frank J. Pintozzi

American Book Company
PO Box 2638
Woodstock, GA 30188-1383
Toll Free: 1 (888) 264-5877   Phone: (770) 928-2834
Fax: (770) 928-7483   Toll Free Fax: 1 (866) 827-3240
www.americanbookcompany.com

ACKNOWLEDGEMENTS

We would like to gratefully acknowledge the formatting and technical contributions of Marsha Torrens and Becky Wright as well as the editing and proofreading contibutions of Mallory Grantham and Susan Barrows.

Copyright© 2010
by American Book Company
PO Box 2638
Woodstock, GA 30188-1318

ALL RIGHTS RESERVED

The text of this publication, or any part thereof, may not be reproduced or transmitted in any form or by any means, electronic or mechanical, including photocopying, recording, storage in an information retrieval system, or otherwise, without the prior written permission of the publisher.

Printed in the United States of America

08/10

Table of Contents

Preface v

Diagnostic Test 1

Chapter 1 Parts of Speech — 23
Nouns 23
Verbs 25
    Verb Tenses 25
Adjectives and Adverbs 27
Chapter Summary 29
Chapter 1 Review 29

Chapter 2 Spelling — 31
Nouns 31
    Regular Nouns 31
    Irregular Nouns 32
Verbs 32
    Regular Verbs 32
    Irregular Verbs 33
Homophones 34
Chapter Summary 36
Chapter 2 Review 36

Chapter 3 Mechanics — 39
End Marks and Abbreviations 39
Commas 41
Capitalization 42
Chapter Summary 44
Chapter 3 Review 45

Chapter 4 Working with Sentences — 47
Subjects and Predicates 47
    Subjects 47
    Predicates 48
    Agreement 49

Variety of Sentences	51
Sentence Structures	51
Sentence Types	52
Fragments	54
Functional Fragments	54
Chapter Summary	56
Chapter 4 Review	57

Chapter 5   Working with Paragraphs   59

What Makes a Good Paragraph?	60
Content	60
Structure	60
Ways to Organize Paragraphs	64
More about Transitions	69
Transitions between Paragraphs	69
Transitional Structures	70
Chapter Summary	74
Chapter 5 Review	74

Chapter 6   Kinds of Writing   79

Types of Writing	79
The Writing Process	80
Prewriting	80
Drafting	81
Choosing a Focus	82
Revising Your Writing	85
Editing Your Writing	89
Publishing	90
Chapter Summary	92
Chapter 6 Review	93

Chapter 7   Research   95

Organizational Features	95
Preface	95
Table of Contents	96
Appendix	96
Glossary	97
Index	97
Using Sources	99
Chapter Summary	103
Chapter 7 Review	104

Practice Test 1	**107**
Practice Test 2	**127**
Index	**147**

Preface

Mastering the Georgia 4th Grade CRCT in English Language Arts will help students who are reviewing for the grade 4 CRCT in English Language Arts. The materials in this book are based on the Georgia GPS standards and other materials published by the Georgia Department of Education. This book is written to the grade 4 reading level and corresponds to 650L to 850L on the Lexile text-measure scale.

This book contains the following sections:

1) General information about the book

2) A diagnostic test

3) A diagnostic evaluation chart

4) Seven chapters that teach the concepts and skills needed for test readiness

5) Two practice tests

Standards are posted at the beginning of each chapter, and they are matched to each question in the diagnostic and practice tests. A chart of standards is included in the teacher's answer manual.

We welcome comments and suggestions about the book. Please contact the authors at

American Book Company
PO Box 2638
Woodstock, GA 30188-1383

Toll Free: 1 (888) 264-5877
Phone: (770) 928-2834
Fax: (770) 928-7483
Web site: www.americanbookcompany.com

Preface

About the Authors

Sara Hinton has a B.A. from Columbia University and an M.A. in the teaching of English from Teachers College, Columbia University. She taught middle school language arts and college courses in writing, grammar, and literature for several years.

Lisa M. Cocca is a former elementary and middle school teacher and librarian. She writes language arts, social studies, and science materials for a wide range of ages.

About the Project Coordinator: **Zuzana Urbanek** serves as ELA Curriculum Coordinator for American Book Company. She is a professional writer with twenty-five years of experience in education, business, and publishing. She has taught a variety of English courses since 1990 at the college level and also taught English as a foreign language abroad. Her master's degree is from Arizona State University.

About the Executive Editor: **Dr. Frank J. Pintozzi** is a former Professor of Education at Kennesaw State University. For over twenty-eight years, he has taught English and reading at the high school and college levels as well as in teacher preparation courses in language arts and social studies. In addition to writing and editing state standard-specific texts for high school exit and end-of-course exams, he has edited and written several college textbooks.

Georgia Grade 4 CRCT ELA Diagnostic Test

The purpose of this diagnostic test is to evaluate your skills in a variety of areas linked to the grade 4 English Language Arts standards published by the Georgia Department of Education.

This test is set up in two sections like the actual CRCT. When you take the CRCT, you have forty-five to seventy minutes to complete each section, with a ten-minute break between them.

GENERAL DIRECTIONS

1 Read all directions carefully.

2 Read each selection.

3 Read each question or example. Then, choose the best answer.

4 Choose only one answer for each question. If you change an answer, be sure to erase the answer completely.

5 At the end of the test, you or your instructor should score your test. Using the evaluation chart following the test, determine whether or not you are prepared for the grade 4 CRCT in English Language Arts. Study the chapters you need to, and then take the practice tests at the back of this book.

Diagnostic Test

Section 1

Georgia Grade 4 CRCT ELA

1. What is the simple subject of the sentence?   4C1a

   > Jill gave the newspaper to her neighbor.

   A Jill
   B gave
   C newspaper
   D her

2. Look at the table of contents. Where will you find information about the Lincoln Memorial?   4W3b

Table of Contents	
Welcome to Washington, D.C.	2
The Washington Memorial	9
The Lincoln Memorial	15
The Vietnam Memorial	22
The Smithsonian	30
The National Zoo	35
The White House	42

   Lincoln Memorial

   A page 2
   B page 9
   C page 15
   D page 30

3. Which sentence uses commas correctly?   4C1c

   A The dog's fur was a mix, of brown, tan and white hairs.
   B The dog's fur was a mix of brown tan and, white hairs.
   C The dog's fur was a mix of brown, tan, and white, hairs.
   D The dog's fur was a mix of brown, tan, and white hairs.

Diagnostic Test

4 Look at the underlined sentence. What change BEST improves the flow of the sentences?   4W1d

> Our town has an Independence Day parade every year. The children in town dress up their bikes. Many groups march or play music. <u>The mayor makes a speech in front of the statue of the soldiers.</u> Later, they show fireworks over the lake. It is always a fun and special day.

- (A) The mayor of our town makes a speech in front of the statue of the soldiers.
- B Seriously, the mayor makes a speech in front of the statue of the soldiers.
- C After the parade, the mayor makes a speech in front of the statue of the soldiers.
- D The mayor makes the same speech in front of the statue of the soldiers each year.

5 The sentence below has a spelling error. Which of the underlined words is spelled incorrectly?   4C1f, 4W4c

> Jenna was <u>honored</u> to <u>axcept</u> the <u>envelope</u> from the <u>committee</u>.

- A honored
- (B) axcept
- C envelope
- D committee

6 How is the paragraph organized?   4W1c

> Ice hockey and street hockey are both alike and different. In both games, players use a hockey stick. The object of both games is to score a goal by getting the game piece past the goalie and into the net. In ice hockey, the game piece is a puck. It is flat and heavy, and it glides across the ice. The players wear ice skates to move on the rink. In street hockey, players wear rollerblades. They hit a small ball with the stick to make a goal.

- (A) compare and contrast
- B time order
- C problem and solution
- D step order

Georgia Grade 4 CRCT ELA

7 Look at the underlined word in each sentence. Which sentence uses the underlined word correctly?   4C1g

   A Lindsey found her books over <u>their</u>.
   B <u>Their</u> looking in the library too.
   C <u>Their</u> are two groups looking for the same books.
   D The second group found <u>their</u> books quickly. ✓

8 Which type of sentence is this?   4C1h

   | I finished my math homework after dinner. |

   A declarative
   B imperative ✓
   C interrogative
   D exclamatory

9 What is the simple predicate of the sentence?   4C1a

   | Yesterday, my older sister swam for hours. |

   A Yesterday
   B my
   C sister
   D swam ✓

10 Which part of speech is the underlined word?   4C1b

   | The red <u>kite</u> stood out against the blue sky. |

   A noun ✓
   B verb
   C adverb
   D adjective

5

Diagnostic Test

11 A student is writing a short biography on Teddy Roosevelt. What kind of organization should the writer use?

- A compare and contrast
- (B) time order
- C problem and solution
- D step order

Teddy Roosevelt

12 Kim is writing a letter to his teacher asking her to stop giving math homework on Fridays. Which sentence would BEST support his argument?

- A I like to spend my weekends having fun.
- B My sister never gets math homework.
- (C) Our class never does the math homework anyway, so it is a waste of your time.
- D Our class could read more on the weekend if we had no math homework on Friday.

13 Which sentence BEST joins the information in the underlined sentences?

> Last summer, I visited the Swiss Alps. <u>Even in the summer, it is cold up on the mountaintop. Because it is cold it is also snowy.</u> I went for a dogsled ride in the deep snow. I also saw an icehouse while I was on the mountaintop. When I came down from the mountain, it was a hot summer day!

- (A) Even in the summer, it is cold and snowy up on the mountaintop.
- B Even in the summer, it is cold and because it is cold, it is also snowy.
- C Even in the summer, it's cold up on the mountaintop and it is also snowy.
- D Even in the summer, up on the mountaintop it's cold and snowy because it's cold.

Georgia Grade 4 CRCT ELA

14 Which is the BEST closing sentence for the paragraph? 4W2Info h

> The American bald eagle is one of our country's symbols. It is our national bird. If Ben Franklin got his way, this would not be true. Franklin wanted the turkey to be our national bird. The Continental Congress didn't like his idea. They decided to come up with a better one.

- A They made the American bald eagle the national bird.
- B They also voted on a seal as a symbol of the country.
- C There is more than one kind of eagle.
- D The American eagle has a white head.

15 Which sentence uses the correct end mark? 4C1c, 4W4c

- A I wonder how he did that?
- B I'm sure it was a simple trick?
- C However, I didn't catch it?
- D Do you know how he did it?

16 Which is a complete sentence? 4C1c

- A The sweet song of the bird in the tree.
- B Ran around the house several times.
- C The fish was hiding among the plants.
- D Sniffing the heavy scent of chocolate.

17 Which choice correctly breaks the sentence between the subject and the predicate? 4C1a

- A My older sister skated / around the ice rink.
- B My older sister / skated around the ice rink.
- C My older / sister skated around the ice rink.
- D My older sister skated around / the ice rink.

7

Diagnostic Test

18 Look at the underlined words in the sentence. Which is spelled incorrectly?

> The <u>scientest</u> and the <u>engineer</u> worked together to <u>develop</u> the new <u>product</u>.

- (A) scientest
- B engineer
- C develop
- D product

19 Which sentence uses the underlined word correctly?

- A I put <u>too</u> teaspoons of mustard in the bowl.
- (B) Jackson thought I had put in <u>too</u> much.
- C I mixed everything and gave him a bit <u>too</u> taste.
- D He wanted me <u>too</u> taste it first!

20 Which part of speech is the underlined word?

> The <u>steel</u> frame of a skyscraper soon filled the once-empty lot.

- A noun
- B verb
- C adverb
- (D) adjective

21 Which underlined word in the sentence should start with a capital letter?

> I sent <u>my</u> <u>aunt</u> Elaine a photo of the <u>road</u> <u>she</u> lives on.

- A my
- (B) aunt
- C road
- D she

Read the glossary.

> **gravel** – a mix of small rocks or pebbles
>
> **mineral** – a solid material taken from the earth
>
> **pebble** – a small rock made smooth by weathering
>
> **property** – something that describes how an item looks, feels, or smells
>
> **rock** – a solid part of Earth made up of minerals
>
> **weathering** – the breaking down of rocks by wind and water

22 Which is a property?

    A   weather   C   stones

    B   color   D   gravel

23 A student is writing a thank-you letter to the school principal. Which sentence works BEST for this purpose?

    A   Thanks a million!

    B   Thanks—you're the man!

    C   Thank you for inviting me to join the committee.

    D   It's about time you invited me to join the committee.

24 Which sentence uses the correct end mark?

    A   Where did Shane buy his new skateboard!

    B   I think he bought it in the new shop downtown!

    C   Look at his new trick!

    D   Can you do that too!

25 Which sentence is written correctly?

    A   The boys is playing basketball.

    B   They is practicing everyday.

    C   We are hoping to win.

    D   The coach are helping us.

Diagnostic Test

26 Which part of speech is the underlined word? 4C1b

| The black horse <u>raced</u> ahead of the others. |

- A   noun
- **B**   verb ✓
- C   adverb
- D   adjective

27 Where is a period needed in the sentence? 4C1c

| Did you give Mr Santiago a note from your doctor yesterday? |

- **A**   after Mr ✓
- B   after Santiago
- C   after doctor
- D   after yesterday

28 Read the sentences. Which underlined word is spelled incorrectly? 4C1f, 4W4c

| First, put the <u>peaches</u> in the <u>baskets</u>. Then put them next to the <u>blueberrys</u> on the front and side <u>porches</u>. |

- A   peaches
- B   baskets
- **C**   blueberrys ✓
- D   porches

29 Which underlined word should start with a capital letter? 4C1c

| Did I leave my favorite book, <u>*thunder*</u>, at your <u>uncle's</u> <u>house</u> or at the <u>library</u>? |

- **A**   thunder ✓
- B   uncle's
- C   house
- D   library

30 What kind of sentence is this? 4C1h

| Is that your mother? |

- A   imperative
- B   declarative
- C   exclamatory
- **D**   interrogative ✓

10

Section 2

Diagnostic Test

31 Which is the complete predicate in the sentence? 4C1a

> The two boys ran quickly across the yard.

    A two boys ran quickly
    B quickly across the yard
    (C) ran quickly across the yard
    D The boys ran quickly across

32 Which sentence uses correct subject-verb agreement? 4C1c

    (A) Chantelle sweeps the porch each morning.
    B The boys sweeps the porch each evening.
    C Val sweep the sidewalks.
    D Rosa never sweep anything!

33 What part of speech is the underlined word? 4C1b

> The <u>bumpy</u> road was difficult to get across.

    A noun
    B verb
    C adverb
    (D) adjective

34 Which sentence uses the correct end mark? 4C1c, 4W4c

    A Would you like to come to my house after school.
    (B) We adopted our dog from the shelter.
    C I want you to meet my great new pet?
    D My dog is very friendly and hardly ever barks?

Georgia Grade 4 CRCT ELA

35 What is the BEST closing sentence for the paragraph? 4W2Narr h

> Nico set up his easel and paints on the back porch. His mother loved the view of the mountains from here. Next week, his mother would celebrate her birthday. Nico hoped he could finish his painting and surprise her with it then.

- A   He really loved to paint.
- B   Nico loved birthdays!
- (C) He knew it would be difficult to keep it a secret for a whole week!
- D   His mother also loved the beach and looking out over the ocean.

36 Which choice correctly places a break between the subject and the predicate? 4C1a

- A   Caroline baked / enough cupcakes for everyone.
- B   Caroline baked enough cupcakes / for everyone.
- (C) Caroline / baked enough cupcakes for everyone.
- D   Caroline baked enough / cupcakes for everyone.

37 Which topic would work BEST for a short essay of three to five paragraphs? 4W1a, 4W4a

- A   sports
- B   American sports
- C   sports that use bats
- (D) the birth of baseball

13

Diagnostic Test

38 What kind of organization does this paragraph use?

> Do you know why Gertrude Ederle is famous? Ederle was the first woman to swim across the English Channel. She achieved this in 1926. This was at a time when women were not seen as real athletes. Ederle changed people's minds. She made it across the waterway while facing strong winds and tides. In fact, she did it faster than the five men who had completed the trip before her!

- A cause and effect
- (B) chronological order
- C question and answer
- D similarity and difference

39 The writer wants to add a sentence to the start of paragraph 2. Which choice would BEST link the paragraphs?

> Benjamin Hawkins held important government jobs. At one time, he was a United States senator. Later, he became the United States agent to the Creek Nation. This job helped keep peace between the United States and the Creek Nation for a long time. He became friends with the Creek chiefs. He supported the tribes in whatever way he could. Hawkins wrote many letters about the Creek people.
>
> We know many Creek communities formed large towns. Others formed groups of small villages. The small villages were settled around a center plaza. The plaza was a center of activity. The people would gather for games, dancing, and ceremonies. Hawkins had close ties with the Creek people. This meant he could give a firsthand account of these things.

- A Hawkins' letters tell us much of what we know about the Creek culture.
- B Benjamin Hawkins received his college education at Princeton University.
- C Hawkins also raised pigs on his farm in what is now northern Georgia.
- (D) Most people living around Hawkins at the time could not read or write.

Georgia Grade 4 CRCT ELA

40 Which sentence is written correctly? 4C1c

    A   Cara and Ava sings beautifully.
    B   The girls sings in the chorus.
    (C)   Cara sings with a theater group too.
    D   They sings all kinds of popular songs.

41 Which is a complete sentence? 4C1c

    A   The sign on the side of the city bus.
    B   In the sun, the glass windows.
    C   Running over, under, and around.
    D   Jason solved a difficult problem.

42 What detail should be added to the paragraph? 4W2Info d

> Have you ever dreamed of growing the world's biggest pumpkin? If so, you have plenty of company. Many growers meet to trade tips. They meet in local groups and on Web sites. They discuss the best soil, food, and seeds. Some even join seed swaps to try to grow bigger pumpkins. Once the pumpkins are grown, they go for an official weigh-in. This takes place at fairs and festivals under the watchful eyes of judges. There are weigh-in locations around the world. This includes the United States, Canada, and many countries in Europe. The record-holding pumpkin was grown in Ohio. It broke a record held for two years by a pumpkin in Massachusetts. That pumpkin only weighed 1,689 pounds!

    A   There are also contests for growing the biggest watermelon.
    B   People often decorate outside with pumpkins in the fall.
    C   Country fairs often hold farm crop and animal contests.
    (D)   The Ohio pumpkin weighed 1,725 pounds on October 3, 2009.

Diagnostic Test

43 What is the BEST place to separate this run-on sentence into two sentences?

> Al works at the pet store he sells tropical fish.

- A after *works*
- (B) after *store*
- C after *sells*
- D after *tropical*

44 What kind of sentence is this?

> Give me a hammer.

- A imperative
- (B) declarative
- C exclamatory
- D interrogative

45 What is the BEST closing sentence for the paragraph?

> Farmers plant peanuts as a cash crop in fifteen different states. First, they till, or turn, the soil. Then, the farmers plant the peanut kernels. This takes place in April or May after the danger of frost passes. About ten days after planting, the new plants sprout. They will grow to be about eighteen inches tall. About forty days after planting, yellow flowers blossom on the plants. Although the flowers grow above ground, the fruit forms under the ground. Two to three months after the plant flowers, the peanuts are ready.

- (A) The farmers pick the peanuts and get them ready to sell.
- B There are many peanut farms in the state of Georgia.
- C Peanuts and peanut oil are used in many different foods.
- D There are many cash crops grown in the United States.

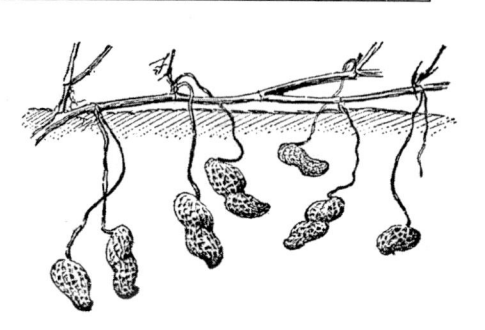

Peanut Plant

16

46 Which sentence would BEST support the information in this paragraph?

> Piper was the bravest person in the book. There were other brave characters in the book, but they were not as brave as Piper. At first, Piper seemed shy. She spoke in a soft voice and had a hard time talking to people she did not know well. Her friends seemed to have no trouble speaking up to everyone. However, when the group faced real danger, it was Piper who kept her head. Her friends stood in harm's way when the twister came through town.

A Piper was also very kind to everyone she knew.
B Piper led her friends to safety in the storm shelter.
C It was the first time a twister had ever come that way.
D A twister is another word people use instead of tornado.

47 Which sentence should be removed from the paragraph?

> ¹ I am most like the main character in the book. ² Atepa loved being outdoors and hiking in the woods. ³ He spent all of his free time exploring the forest near his village. ⁴ I love the outdoors too. ⁵ I spend almost every Saturday hiking in the woods behind my house. ⁶ I also love to go to movies based on the books I read.

A sentence 3
B sentence 4
C sentence 5
D sentence 6

Diagnostic Test

48 What is the BEST closing sentence for the paragraph? 4W2Lit f

> In this book, Simon and Elizabeth were most alike. Both were loyal friends. Simon's best friend broke a promise to the secret club. Simon stood by his friend when the others became angry with him. Elizabeth wanted to go to the movie with the girls. When her best friend broke her leg, Elizabeth skipped the movie. She visited with her friend instead. Both characters were also very responsible. Simon's friends agreed to help clean the park. When the grown-ups left, the boys stopped working. Simon finished picking up the trash, even though no one was watching. Elizabeth also faced a problem like that. Elizabeth and her sister promised to take care of a neighbor's puppy. Her sister quit after one day. Elizabeth finished the job by herself.

A   However, Elizabeth loved playing basketball, and Simon loved playing baseball.
B   Elizabeth was also very much like Margaret, the other girl in the movie club.
C   Simon and Elizabeth had many of the same strengths.
D   Simon was at least six inches taller than Elizabeth.

49 A student wants to add the following sentence to the paragraph. 4W4b

The green layer of the chestnut is removed before it is cooked.

Where in the paragraph does the sentence belong?

> [1] The American chestnut tree can grow to be one hundred feet tall. [2] When it blooms, it is covered in small white flowers. [3] Later the fruit, the chestnut, forms. [4] The nut is covered by a thick green skin with sharp thorns. [5] The chestnuts are later eaten by people and by animals.

A   after sentence 1
B   after sentence 2
C   after sentence 3
D   after sentence 4

Georgia Grade 4 CRCT ELA

50 Katie is writing a list of the resources she used for her report. Which entry includes all of the needed information?

- **A** Smith, Lynn. <u>National Monuments</u>. Boston: ABC Press, 2009.
- B Jones, Greg. <u>The Lincoln and Washington Memorials</u>. Chicago, 2007.
- C Garcia, Jose. <u>Washington, D.C.: A City of Monuments</u>. Lincoln Press, 2010.
- D Cho, Ku-San. <u>A Capitol Idea</u>. New York: Apple Press, Park Elementary Library, 2005.

51 Tamika is looking in the dictionary for the definition of *swarm*. What guidewords should she look for on the top of the page?

- A snort / stagger
- **B** succeed / sweater
- C swim / syllable
- D shift / skim

52 In which sentence is the underlined word used correctly?

- A I used leftover <u>would</u> to build the doghouse.
- **B** <u>Would</u> you like to help me paint it?
- C We <u>wood</u> do it this afternoon.
- D I think you <u>wood</u> do a great job!

53 Which is a compound sentence?

- A I bought milk and bread at the store.
- **B** I made lunch, and I washed the dishes.
- C Mary and Deb came over.
- D They brought dessert.

19

Diagnostic Test

54 Read the sentence below. Which choice corrects the mistake in the sentence?   4C1c

> My friend Molly attends the Washington Middle school in Georgia.

   A   My Friend Molly attends the Washington Middle school in Georgia.
   B   My friend Molly attends the Washington middle school in Georgia.
   C   My friend Molly attends the washington middle school in Georgia.
   D   My friend Molly attends the Washington Middle School in Georgia.

55 What is the complete subject in the sentence below?   4C1a

> My youngest brother reads books about history.

   A   brother
   B   My brother
   C   My youngest brother
   D   My youngest brother reads

56 Which sentence BEST supports the main idea of the paragraph?   4W2Per c

> Fourth graders should be allowed to eat lunch outside. The school lunchroom is too crowded and noisy. The school has picnic tables that are never used. Using the picnic tables will mean more open seats in the school lunchroom.

   A   Fourth graders are old enough; they should be able to use the picnic tables.
   B   The school should also improve the food; the salads are always soggy.
   C   The picnic tables could use a fresh coat of paint.
   D   I am a fourth grader who wants to eat outside.

57 Which choice is a functional fragment?   4C1h

   A   Yes!
   B   Like Margaret.
   C   When will?
   D   Sleeps.

58 What part of speech is the underlined word? 4C1b

> Max spoke <u>quietly</u> in the library.

- A noun
- B verb
- (C) adverb
- D adjective

59 Which is the BEST closing sentence for the paragraph? 4W2Per f

> Vote for me for class president. I promise to be fair and honest with everyone. I will work hard and attend all meetings. I have good grades, I am always on time, and I work well with others.

- A I am already president of the art club.
- B I am running against Nathaniel Daniels.
- C I will do a great job for you if you vote for me.
- D I also have a puppy, which shows I'm responsible.

60 Which is an example of computer software? 4W3d

- (A) a printer
- B a monitor
- C a keyboard
- D a publishing CD

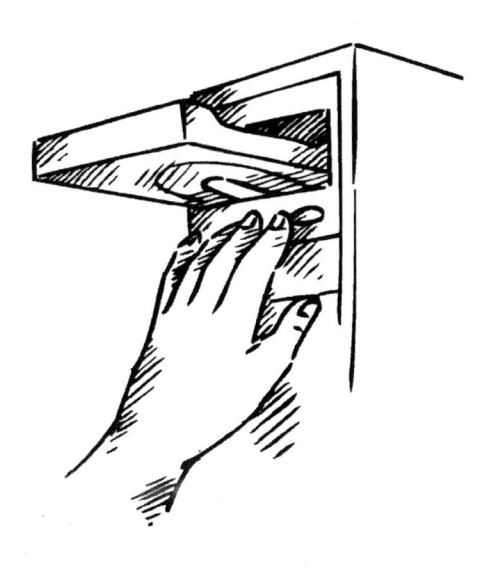

EVALUATION CHART FOR GEORGIA 4TH GRADE CRCT IN ENGLISH LANGUAGE ARTS DIAGNOSTIC TEST

Directions: On the following chart, circle the question numbers that you answered incorrectly and evaluate the results. Then turn to the appropriate chapters, read the explanations, and complete the exercises. Review other chapters as needed. Finally, complete the practice tests to assess your progress and further prepare you for the **Georgia 4th Grade CRCT in ELA**.

Note: Some question numbers will appear under multiple chapters because those questions require demonstration of multiple skills.

Chapters	Diagnostic Test Questions
Chapter 1: Parts of Speech	10, 20, 26, 33, 58
Chapter 2: Spelling	5, 7, 18, 19, 28, 52
Chapter 3: Mechanics	3, 15, 21, 24, 25, 27, 29, 32, 34, 40, 43, 54
Chapter 4: Working with Sentences	1, 8, 9, 16, 17, 30, 31, 36, 41, 44, 53, 55, 57
Chapter 5: Working with Paragraphs	4, 6, 11, 12, 13, 14, 23, 35, 37, 38, 39, 42, 45, 46, 47, 48, 49, 56, 59
Chapter 6: Kinds of Writing	5, 11, 15, 18, 24, 28, 34, 37
Chapter 7: Research	2, 22, 50, 51, 60

Chapter 1
Parts of Speech

This chapter covers the following Georgia CRCT standard and benchmark:

> **ELA4C1:** The student demonstrates understanding and control of the rules of the English language, realizing that usage involves the appropriate application of conventions and grammar in both written and spoken formats. The student
>
> **b.** Uses and identifies four basic parts of speech (adjective, noun, verb, adverb).

Words are a big part of everyday life. You can find words on cereal boxes, billboards, and in school books. When you write, you use words in different ways. Part of understanding how to use a word is understanding what part of speech it is. Parts of speech tell what a word is and how to use it. When you know what part of speech a word is, you can use it correctly when you write.

There are many **parts of speech**. The parts of speech covered in this chapter are nouns, verbs, adjectives, and adverbs.

NOUNS

A **noun** is a person, place, thing, or idea. The chart below shows some examples of nouns.

Noun	Examples
person	baby, Aunt Reba, president
place	Macon, beach, moon
thing	fork, cell phone, money
idea	celebration, love, freedom

Nouns can be proper or common.

A **proper noun** names a specific thing. Proper nouns are always capitalized.

Some examples of proper nouns are *Jekyll Island*, *Fred*, and *Microsoft*.

Parts of Speech

A **common noun** names a general thing. Common nouns are not capitalized unless they are part of a title or at the beginning of a sentence.

Some examples of common nouns are *chocolate*, *shower*, and *tent*.

Here are some nouns used in sentences. The nouns are shown in bold.

The **kitten** chased the **yarn** into the **bedroom**.

Ms. Norris handed out **scissors** to the **class**.

The **explorer**'s **fear** was understandable.

Practice 1: Nouns

Which word in each sentence is a noun?

1. My ice cream fell on the floor!
   A   My   B   ice cream   C   on   D   fell

2. Without bravery, the war will be lost.
   A   will   B   the   C   bravery   D   Without

3. In January, school was cancelled because it snowed.
   A   January   B   because   C   snowed   D   was

4. When this bike wears out, can I get a new one?
   A   When   B   bike   C   this   D   new

5. The cold water made his hands turn blue.
   A   cold   B   hands   C   blue   D   turn

24

Chapter 1

VERBS

A **verb** is an action word. A verb tells what happens in a sentence.

Some examples of verbs are *bake*, *listen*, *walk*, and *hunt*.

A verb can show action, as in this sentence.

    Example: The shaggy lion **bit** the smaller lion.

A verb can also show a state of being, as in this sentence.

    Example: The shaggy lion **is** fierce.

VERB TENSES

Verbs describe action that is happening now, action that has already happened, or action that will happen. **Verb tenses** tell when the action is happening. Some common verb tenses are present, past, and future. The chart below shows how the regular verbs look in each of these tenses.

Verb Tenses—Regular	Tense	Description	Examples
to chew, to believe, to ask	Present	action that is happening now or happens all the time	he chews, he believes, he asks
to chew, to believe, to ask	Past	action that already happened and has ended	he chewed, he believed, he asked
to chew, to believe, to ask	Future	action that has not yet happened	he will chew, he will believe, he will ask

Notice how all of these verbs act the same when they change tense. For example, all of these verbs end in *ed* in the past tense.

25

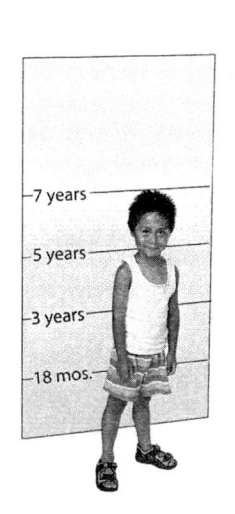

Parts of Speech

Some verbs do not follow these rules. **Irregular verbs** do not always follow the pattern when changing tense that you saw on page 25.

Verb Tenses—Irregular	Tense	Description	Examples
to sing, to eat, to buy	Present	action that is happening now or happens all the time	he sings, he eats, he buys
to sing, to eat, to buy	Past	action that already happened and has ended	he sang, he ate, he bought
to sing, to eat, to buy	Future	action that has not yet happened	he will sing, he will eat, he will buy

Notice that some verb tenses have more than one word. For example, the future tense of the verb *to chew* is *will chew*. Include all parts of a verb when you identify a verb.

> **Example:** Elsa *has grown* two inches since last month.

The verb in this sentence is *has grown*. You would need to include both words when you identify the verb.

Practice 2: Verbs

Which word in each sentence is a verb?

1. Have you ever ridden a horse?
    - A you
    - B horse
    - C ever
    - D ridden

2. Eating cake for breakfast made Crystal sick.
    - A cake
    - B breakfast
    - C made
    - D Crystal

Chapter 1

3 **My grandfather lost his glasses.**

   A glasses   C my

   B lost   D his

4 **Jed's mom bakes the best brownies.**

   A Jed's   C brownies

   B bakes   D best

5 **The gardeners will work when it is light outside.**

   A will work   C gardeners

   B work   D when

ADJECTIVES AND ADVERBS

Adjectives and adverbs give extra information about other words in a sentence.

An **adjective** describes a noun. It tells what kind or how many. Examples of adjectives are *cold*, *scary*, *green*, and *fifty*.

Here are some adjectives used in sentences. The adjectives are shown in bold.

   The **smelly** rat was covered in **gooey** slime.

   Patti brought **three** fossils to show the **science** class.

An **adverb** usually describes a verb. An adverb tells "when" and "how." Examples of adverbs are *rudely*, *quickly*, and *sometimes*.

Fossil of a Fish

Here are some adverbs used in sentences. The adverbs are shown in bold.

   How **quickly** can you finish these math problems?

   Paul **always** brings grapes in his lunch.

Using adjectives and adverbs in your writing help make it more interesting. When you use colorful adjectives and adverbs, your reader will see a clearer picture of what you are writing about.

Parts of Speech

Practice 3: Adjectives and Adverbs

Which word in each sentence is an adjective?

1. The twins recycled the ripped paper.
   - A twins
   - B paper
   - C recycled
   - D ripped

2. Royce just ran his longest race ever.
   - A ran
   - B longest
   - C Royce
   - D race

3. Without loud sirens, smoke detectors do not work correctly.
   - A loud
   - B correctly
   - C work
   - D detectors

Which word in each sentence is an adverb?

4. Jorge happily put the last piece of the puzzle in place.
   - A put
   - B happily
   - C place
   - D of

5. Nick's baby sister wailed loudly from her crib.
   - A crib
   - B wailed
   - C loudly
   - D baby

6. The crowd waited patiently for the speech to begin.
   - A The
   - B speech
   - C waited
   - D patiently

Chapter 1

> ## CHAPTER SUMMARY
>
> **Parts of speech** tell how to use words correctly when you are writing.
>
> A **noun** is a person, place, thing, or idea.
>
> A **verb** is an action word.
>
> **Adjectives** and **adverbs** give extra information about other words in a sentence. These parts of speech can make writing come alive.

CHAPTER 1 REVIEW

What is the underlined word in each sentence?

1. The biggest mountain near my house is <u>Stone Mountain</u>.

    A noun
    B verb
    C adjective
    D adverb

2. The waiter <u>served</u> us dinner.

    A noun
    B verb
    C adjective
    D adverb

    Stone Mountain, GA

3. My uncle takes me fishing on <u>sunny</u> days.

    A noun   C adjective
    B verb   D adverb

4. May I borrow that <u>cardboard</u> box?

    A noun   C adjective
    B verb   D adverb

29

Parts of Speech

5 Jessie always brings an <u>orange</u> for lunch.

    (A) noun
    B   verb
    C   adjective
    D   adverb

6 Please <u>wash</u> your hands before dinner.

A	noun	C	adjective
(B)	verb	D	adverb

7 John <u>correctly</u> answered the question.

A	noun	C	adjective
B	verb	(D)	adverb

8 Talk <u>quietly</u> in the movie theater.

A	noun	C	adjective
B	verb	(D)	adverb

9 It is my job to <u>bring</u> papers to the office this week.

A	noun	C	adjective
(B)	verb	D	adverb

10 <u>Hot</u> cheese burns the roof of my mouth.

A	noun	(C)	adjective
B	verb	D	adverb

Chapter 2
Spelling

This chapter covers the following Georgia CRCT standard and benchmarks:

> **ELA4C1:** The student demonstrates understanding and control of the rules of the English language, realizing that usage involves the appropriate application of conventions and grammar in both written and spoken formats. The student
>
> **f.** Uses knowledge of letter sounds, word parts, word segmentation, and syllabication to monitor and correct spelling.
>
> **g.** Spells most commonly used homophones correctly (there, they're, their; two, too, to).

Spelling is an important part of writing. You need to spell words correctly so your reader can understand you. Misspelled words can distract a reader. You can make it easy for your reader to tell what you are saying by spelling words correctly.

NOUNS

There are some common **spelling rules** that most **nouns** follow. Here are some rules for making nouns plural.

REGULAR NOUNS

To make most **regular nouns** plural, add *s*.

> **Examples:**
> season + s = seasons
> icicle + s = icicles

To make nouns that end with *s, z, x, sh,* or *ch* plural, add *es*.

> **Examples:**
> circus + es = circuses
> porch + es = porches

To make nouns that end in a consonant + *y* plural, change the *y* to *i* and add *es*.

> **Examples:**
> gallery – y + ies = galleries
> century – y + ies = centuries

31

Irregular Nouns

Some words do not follow these rules. These words are irregular. **Irregular nouns** do not follow the rules when changing from singular to plural. Some nouns keep the same spelling in the plural, like the word *fish*. Others change spelling completely. For irregular nouns, you will need to memorize the plural form. Here are some examples.

Irregular Noun Plurals	
Singular	**Plural**
child	children
deer	deer
foot	feet
man	men
ox	oxen
sheep	sheep
woman	women

Verbs

Like nouns, most **verbs** follow common spelling rules when they change tense.

Regular Verbs

To form the past tense of most **regular verbs**, add *ed*.

Examples:

caution + *ed* = cautioned
stretch + *ed* = stretched

To form the past tense of verbs that end with silent *e*, drop the *e*, then add *ed*.

Examples:

argue − *e* + *ed* = argued
serve − *e* + *ed* = served

Chapter 2

RULES

IRREGULAR VERBS

Like some nouns, some verbs do not follow these common spelling rules. You learned in chapter 1 that these are **irregular verbs**. For irregular verbs, memorize the past tense.

| Irregular Verb Past Tense ||
Present	Past
begin	began
overhear	overheard
rebuild	rebuilt
seek	sought

Practice 1: Spelling Nouns and Verbs

Each sentence below has a spelling error. Which of the underlined words is spelled incorrectly?

1 How many <u>animales</u> have you <u>counted</u> in the <u>largest</u> <u>corral</u>?
   A animales   C largest
   B count   D corral

2 Jed and Anna <u>took</u> <u>sandwichs</u> on the <u>afternoon</u> <u>hike</u>.
   A took   C afternoon
   B sandwichs   D hike

3 Our <u>teachers</u> <u>informd</u> us that Thursday and Friday <u>would</u> be school <u>holidays</u>.
   A teachers   C would
   B informd   D holidays

4 I'm <u>surprised</u> the <u>fish</u> <u>have</u> not <u>spolid</u> by now.
   A surprised   C have
   B fish   D spolid

33

RULES Spelling

5 How many <u>centurys</u> have the <u>dinosaur</u> <u>bones</u> <u>laid</u> there?

    Ⓐ centurys   C bones

    B dinosaur   D laid

6 While Mr. Roberts <u>corrected</u> <u>papers</u>, the <u>class</u> did math <u>problemes</u>.

    A corrected   B papers   C class   Ⓓ problemes

7 These <u>gentlemans</u> <u>looked</u> like they <u>could</u> use some <u>help</u>.

    Ⓐ gentlemans   C could

    B looked   D help

8 <u>Crowing</u> <u>roosteres</u> might wake <u>people</u> <u>visiting</u> a farm.

    Ⓐ Crowing   B roosteres   C people   D visiting

HOMOPHONES

Homophones are words that sound the same but have different meanings. They can also have different spellings. So, it is important to use the right one. If you know the meaning of a homophone, you can use it correctly when you write. For example, words with an apostrophe are actually made of two words. This means that *you're* stands for "you are." Keep this in mind when choosing the right homophone. Look up other homophones in the dictionary or on the Internet.

Some Common Homophones	
close, clothes	weak, week
there, their, they're	whose, who's
to, too, two	would, wood
threw, through	your, you're

If you don't know the meaning of one of the homophones above, look it up in your dictionary.

It is important to use the correct homophone when you write so that your reader understands what you mean.

Chapter 2

Practice 2: Homophones

Choose the correct homophone for each sentence.

1. Did Jamila eat the ____ pizza by herself?
   - A whole
   - B hole

2. The Jacksons took ____ new car on vacation.
   - A there
   - B they're
   - C their

3. If we stop at the store on the way home, I can ____ milk.
   - A by
   - B buy

4. Mom bought ____ many favors for the party.
   - A to
   - B two
   - C too

5. That construction worker just tripped over a ____!
   - A board
   - B bored

6. After she nearly fell off her bike, Marissa looked a little ____
   - A pail
   - B pale

RULES
Spelling

> ## CHAPTER SUMMARY
>
> Use correct **spelling** when you write to make your meaning clear.
>
> Most words follow common spelling rules.
>
> To make most **regular nouns** plural, add *s* or *es*. For nouns that end with a consonant + *y* plural, change the *y* to *i* and add *es*. **Irregular nouns** have different spellings that you need to memorize.
>
> To form the past tense of most **regular verbs**, add *d* or *ed*. **Irregular verbs** have different endings in the past tense, which you will need to learn.
>
> **Homophones** are words that sound alike but have different meanings and often are not spelled alike. Make sure you learn their meanings so you can use the correct word in the right place.

CHAPTER 2 REVIEW

Each sentence below has a spelling error. Choose the underlined word that is spelled incorrectly.

1. Are you and <u>your</u> <u>sisters</u> <u>aloud</u> to play that <u>video</u> game?

    A   your
    B   sisters
    C   aloud
    D   video

2. "<u>Look</u> at the <u>giant</u> <u>octopus</u>!" Liam <u>exclaimd</u>.

    A   Look
    B   giant
    C   octopus
    D   exclaimd

36

Chapter 2

3 Marshall <u>watched</u> the dog <u>bury</u> <u>it's</u> bone in the <u>backyard</u>.

   A watched
   B bury
   C it's
   D backyard

4 There is a lot of <u>racket</u> <u>coming</u> from that <u>cage</u> of <u>canarys</u>.

   A racket
   B coming
   C cage
   D canarys

5 <u>Soldieres</u> are <u>stationed</u> on <u>every</u> <u>battleship</u>.

   A Soldieres
   B stationed
   C every
   D battleship

6 By the <u>time</u> Maisy <u>arrived</u> in the <u>cafeteria</u>, <u>lunch</u> was over.

   A time
   B arrived
   C cafeteria
   D lunch

7 Geese <u>groom</u> <u>they're</u> <u>feathers</u> to keep <u>themselves</u> clean.

   A groom
   B they're
   C feathers
   D themselves

8 Jon <u>used</u> one cup of <u>cranberrys</u> when he <u>prepared</u> <u>dessert</u>.

   A used
   B cranberrys
   C prepared
   D dessert

RULES

Spelling

9 We'll need a <u>ladder</u> to trim the <u>dead</u> <u>branchs</u> from that <u>tree</u>.

    A ladder
    B dead
    (C) branchs
    D tree

10 Ramon <u>emptyed</u> the bag of different <u>candies</u> into the <u>bowl</u> on the teacher's <u>desk</u>.

    (A) emptyed
    B candies
    C bowl
    D desk

Chapter 3
Mechanics

This chapter covers the following Georgia CRCT standard and benchmark:

ELA4C1: The student demonstrates understanding and control of the rules of the English language, realizing that usage involves the appropriate application of conventions and grammar in both written and spoken formats. The student
c. Uses and identifies correct mechanics (end marks, commas for series, capitalization) ….

Mechanics is the use of punctuation and capitalization in a sentence. Using punctuation marks and capital letters in the right places makes your meaning clear. It also helps you add emotion to your writing. When you use correct mechanics, your reader will understand what you want to say and how you want to say it.

END MARKS AND ABBREVIATIONS

End marks are the punctuation marks at the end of a sentence. Periods, question marks, and exclamation points are all end marks.

Which end mark you use depends on what the sentence says and how it says it.

Use **exclamation points** to show emotion.

> **Examples:**
> Quick, bring me the fire extinguisher!
> I can't believe we won!

Use **question marks** to ask a direct question.

> **Examples:**
> Can you believe they built another shopping plaza?
> Why did Zoltan crumple his paper?

Note: For indirect questions, do not use a question mark. Use a period. **Example:** Shane asked if I could believe that they built another shopping plaza.

Mechanics

Use **periods** to make a statement or to give instructions.

> **Examples:**
> You can sign up for band tryouts on Monday.
> Please set the table.

In addition to ending most sentences, periods are also used for **abbreviations**.

> **Examples:**
> U.S.A.
> 6:00 a.m.
> Dr. Fuller
> St. Joseph's Hospital

Practice 1: End Marks and Abbreviations

Which mark is the BEST to end each sentence?

1. Please help me find the way to the office
   - (A) .
   - B !
   - C ?
   - D ,

2. Do you have a favorite TV show
   - A .
   - B !
   - (C) ?
   - D ,

3. Help, my boat is sinking
   - A .
   - (B) !
   - C ?
   - D ,

4. Ethan took a taxi across town
   - (A) .
   - B !
   - C ?
   - D ,

5. I think the danger has passed
   - (A) .
   - B !
   - C ?
   - D ,

6. Where can I find fishing tackle
   - A .
   - B !
   - (C) ?
   - D ,

Chapter 3

COMMAS

Commas are punctuation marks used within a sentence. They can separate ideas or parts of a sentence. There are many ways to use commas in your writing. Here are some common ways to use commas.

Use a comma to separate the day from the year in a date.

>**Example:** April 2, 2000

Use a comma to separate a city and state.

>**Example:** Vidalia, Georgia

Use a comma between items in a series.

>**Example:** Michael, Sydney, and Jamal walked home together.

Use a comma in a direct address.

>**Example:** Can I play soccer this season, Mom?

Use a comma after the greeting in a letter.

>**Example:** Dear Aunt Susan,

Use a comma after the closing of a letter.

>**Example:** Love, Jamie

Practice 2: Commas

Choose the sentence that uses commas correctly.

1.   A   The class took a field trip to Atlanta, Georgia.
        B   The class, took a field trip to Atlanta Georgia.
        C   The class, took a field trip to Atlanta, Georgia.
        D   The class took a field trip, to Atlanta Georgia.

2.   A   Dad can I have a snack?
        B   Dad can I have, a snack?
        C   Dad, can I have a snack?
        D   Dad, can I have, a snack?

Mechanics

3 A Ana likes cheese sausage and peppers on her pizza.
    (B) Ana likes cheese, sausage, and peppers on her pizza.
    C Ana likes cheese sausage and peppers, on her pizza.
    D Ana, likes cheese sausage, and peppers on her pizza.

4 (A) My birthday party will be on October 8, 2010.
    B My birthday party will be on, October 8, 2010.
    C My birthday party will be on October 8 2010.
    D My birthday party, will be on October 8, 2010.

5 (A) Do you want to go fishing, next weekend Grant?
    B Do you want to go fishing, next weekend, Grant?
    C Do you want to go fishing next weekend Grant?
    D Do you want to go fishing next weekend, Grant?

6 A We need to take along good, walking shoes, a flashlight, and bug spray.
    (B) We need to take along good walking shoes, a flashlight, and bug spray.
    C We need to take along good walking shoes a flashlight, and bug spray.
    D We need to take along good walking shoes, a flashlight and, bug spray.

CAPITALIZATION

The first letter of some words is capitalized. Sometimes, a word needs a capital letter in one sentence but not in another. Read on to learn when to use **capitalization**.

Capitalize the first word of a sentence.

    Example: Spring is my favorite season.

Capitalize "I" when you are talking about yourself.

    Example: When I feel excited, I often dance.

Capitalize days of the week and months of the year.

    Example: This year, August 22 falls on a Sunday.

Chapter 3

Capitalize languages.

Example: In sixth grade, I will start taking Chinese.

Capitalize proper nouns.

Example: My mom's brother, Uncle Martin, is a scientist.

> Only capitalize *uncle* and other relationship names if they are part of a name or if they stand in for a name.
>
> **Examples:**
> I went shopping with Aunt Rosie.
> I went shopping with my aunt.

Capitalize titles.

Example: When was Senator Isakson elected?

Capitalize proper adjectives. You learned in chapter 1 that adjectives describe nouns. A **proper adjective** is formed from a proper noun.

For example, *France* is a noun. *French* is the proper adjective.

Example: Tarts are my favorite French pastries.

Practice 3: Capitalization

In questions 1 through 5, choose the sentence that uses capitalization correctly.

1. A. The american coast is rocky and wild where I live.
   B. The American Coast is rocky and wild where I live.
   C. The American coast is rocky and wild where I live.
   D. The American coast is Rocky and Wild where I live.

2. A. I have an appointment with Dr. Wagner.
   B. I have an appointment with dr. Wagner.
   C. I have an appointment with dr. wagner.
   D. i have an appointment with Dr. Wagner.

Mechanics

3. A. Alec and Matt went surfing with their Uncle.
   B. Alec and matt went surfing with their uncle.
   C. Alec and Matt went Surfing with their Uncle.
   D. Alec and Matt went surfing with their uncle.

4. A. Janey broke her leg on tuesday, May 4.
   B. Janey broke her leg on Tuesday, May 4.
   C. Janey broke her leg on tuesday, may 4.
   D. janey broke her leg on Tuesday, may 4.

5. A. President obama was elected in November of 2008.
   B. president obama was elected in November of 2008.
   C. President Obama was elected in november of 2008.
   D. President Obama was elected in November of 2008.

CHAPTER SUMMARY

End marks are the punctuation marks at the end of a sentence.

Use **exclamation points** to show emotion.

Use **question marks** to ask questions.

Use **periods** to make a statement, to give instructions, and for abbreviations.

Commas separate ideas in a sentence. Commas can separate dates, places, items in a series, and parts of a letter.

Use **capital** letters at the start of a sentence, with proper nouns, and with proper adjectives.

Chapter 3

CHAPTER 3 REVIEW

In questions 1 through 10, choose the sentence that uses mechanics correctly.

1.
   A. Caroline asked if I could come to her house on Tuesday!
   B. Caroline asked if I could come to her house on Tuesday?
   C. Caroline asked if I could come to her house on Tuesday.
   D. Caroline asked if, I could come to her house on Tuesday.

2.
   A. I go back to school on Monday, august 23.
   B. I go back to school on monday, August 23.
   C. I go back to school on Monday August 23.
   D. I go back to school on Monday, August 23.

3.
   A. My family has gone to this baptist Church since I was born.
   B. My family has gone to this baptist church since I was born.
   C. My family has gone to this Baptist church since I was born.
   D. My Family has gone to this Baptist church since I was born.

4.
   A. Will Samantha be singing in the glee club?
   B. Will Samantha be singing in the glee club.
   C. Will Samantha be singing, in the glee club?
   D. Will Samantha be singing in the glee club!

5.
   A. Jake gets home from school at 3:00 pm
   B. Jake gets home from school at 3:00 p.m.
   C. Jake gets home, from school at 3:00 p.m.
   D. Jake gets home from school, at 3:00 p.m.

6.
   A. The nurse asked dr weil for advice.
   B. The nurse asked Dr. Weil for advice.
   C. The nurse asked Dr. weil for advice.
   D. The Nurse asked Dr. Weil for advice.

45

Mechanics

7 A Jenna, I would like you to fold the Towels.
   B Jenna, i would like you to fold the towels.
   C Jenna I would like you to fold the towels.
   D Jenna, I would like you to fold the towels.

8 A Did you read about the blizzard in Portsmouth New Hampshire?
   B Did you read about the Blizzard in Portsmouth, New Hampshire?
   C Did you read about the blizzard in Portsmouth, New Hampshire?
   D Did you read about the blizzard in portsmouth, new hampshire.

9 A I think English is the easiest language to learn.
   B I think english is the easiest language to learn.
   C i think English is the easiest language to learn.
   D I think English is the easiest Language to learn.

10 A Chloe's aunt is going to pick her up after school.
   B Chloe's Aunt is going to pick her up after school.
   C Chloe's aunt, is going to pick her up after school.
   D Chloe's aunt is going to pick her up, after school.

Chapter 4
Working with Sentences

This chapter covers the following Georgia CRCT standard and benchmarks:

ELA4C1: The student demonstrates understanding and control of the rules of the English language, realizing that usage involves the appropriate application of conventions and grammar in both written and spoken formats. The student
a. Recognizes the subject-predicate relationship in sentences.
c. Uses and identifies ... correct usage (subject and verb agreement in a simple sentence), and correct sentence structure (elimination of sentence fragments).
h. Varies the sentence structure by kind (declarative, interrogative, imperative, and exclamatory sentences and functional fragments), order, and complexity (simple, compound).

A sentence is a complete thought. It tells who is doing what. There are several different types of sentences. Understanding what makes a sentence and how to use different kinds of sentences makes your writing both correct and interesting to read.

SUBJECTS AND PREDICATES

SUBJECTS

A **subject** is who (or what) the sentence is about. To find the subject of a sentence, there are a few simple steps to take.

To find the subject of a sentence

    Step 1:   Find the verb.

    Step 2:   Put *who* or *what* in front of the verb.

The answer is the subject.

        Example: Jordan rolled the ball to the baby.

    Step 1:   In this sentence, the verb is *rolled*.

    Step 2:   Ask "Who rolled?"

The answer is *Jordan,* so Jordan is the subject of the sentence.

Working with Sentences

Now you try it with the sentence below.

> Dad is watching my game tonight.

Step 1: What is the verb?

(If you said *is watching*, you're right!)

Step 2: Next, ask the question.

(If you said, "Who is watching?" you're right!)

What is the subject?

(If you said *Dad*, you're right!)

A **simple subject** is just the person or thing doing the action.

A **complete subject** is all of the words that tell about the subject.

> **Example:** Six hungry wolves trotted out of the woods.

Wolves is the simple subject. *Six* and *hungry* both describe wolves, so the complete subject is *six hungry wolves*.

PREDICATES

A **predicate** tells about the subject. The predicate might tell what the subject is doing or what happens to the subject.

A **simple predicate** is just the verb.

> **Examples:**
> Emma's dog chased the ball.
> The crowd waved flags.

A **complete predicate** is the verb and the words that go with it.

> **Examples:**
> Emma's dog chased the ball.
> The crowd waved flags.

Chapter 4

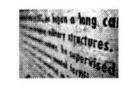

AGREEMENT

Subjects and verbs in a sentence must agree. This is called **subject-verb agreement**, and it means that if the subject is singular, the verb must be singular. *Singular* means "one." If the subject is plural, the verb must be plural. *Plural* means "more than one."

The subject is usually a noun. You learned about making nouns plural in chapter 2. To make a subject plural, you will usually add *s*.

Example: *kid* (singular) becomes *kids* (plural)

To make a verb plural, you will usually take away the *s*.

Example: *kicks* (singular) becomes *kick* (plural)
The <u>kid kicks</u> the ball.
The <u>kids kick</u> the ball.

When deciding if the subject and verb agree, look at the subject first. Once you know if the subject is singular or plural, make the verb match.

Example: The white <u>horse wins</u> the race!

The subject is singular, so the verb must be singular to match. *Horse* and *wins* are both singular, so the sentence is correct.

Example: Several <u>horses win</u> every day.

The subject is plural, so the verb must be plural to match. *Horses* and *win* are both plural, so the sentence is correct.

Practice 1: Subjects and Predicates

1 **What is the subject in the sentence?**

> The computer is not working today.

- (A) computer
- B is
- C working
- D today

49

Working with Sentences

2. What is the underlined part of this sentence?

   <u>Sheila and her friends</u> like to go window-shopping at the mall.

   A   simple subject
   B   complete subject
   C   simple predicate
   D   complete predicate

3. What is the subject in the sentence?

   The bus stopped at the crowded corner.

   A   bus
   B   stopped
   C   crowded
   D   corner

4. What is the simple predicate in the sentence?

   A man paused to put on his gloves.

   A   man
   B   paused
   C   his
   D   gloves

5. Which sentence shows correct subject-verb agreement?

   A   The crows pick at the corn.
   B   The crows picks at the corn.
   C   The crow picking at the corn.
   D   The crow pick at the corn.

Chapter 4

6 What change should be made in this sentence?

| Sonja work with clay in art class. |

   A   Sonja work with clay in art classes.
   B   Sonja is work with clay in art class.
   C   Sonja is works with clay in art class.
   (D) Sonja works with clay in art class.

7 What is the simple predicate in the sentence?

| Three geese flew silently overhead. |

   A   Three
   B   geese
   (C) flew
   D   overhead

8 What is the complete subject in this sentence?

| The dog's leash got wrapped around a tree. |

   A   dog
   B   leash
   (C) The dog's leash
   D   The dog's leash got wrapped

VARIETY OF SENTENCES

There are many kinds of sentences you can use when you are writing. Using a **variety of sentences** makes writing more interesting to read.

SENTENCE STRUCTURES

A **simple sentence** has a subject and a verb. It expresses a complete thought.

      Example: Most chicks are born in the spring.

A **compound sentence** is two or more simple sentences joined by a comma and a word like *and*, *but*, or *so*.

      Example: The batter slid into home, and the crowd cheered.

Working with Sentences

SENTENCE TYPES

There are different types of sentences. Each type also can be simple or compound.

An **imperative** sentence gives a command.

> **Examples:**
> Bring the potatoes to the table.
> Take off your shoes, and go wash your hands.

A **declarative** sentence makes a statement.

> **Examples:**
> A robin is at the bird feeder.
> We took a test in math class today, and I got a B.

An **exclamatory** sentence shows strong feeling and ends with an exclamation point.

> **Examples:**
> Look out for the rockslide!
> Yikes, that car almost hit a pole!

An **interrogative** sentence asks a question and ends with a question mark.

> **Examples:**
> How did James do that magic trick?
> Why did you leave, and where did you go?

Chapter 4

Practice 2: Variety of Sentences

Which type of sentence is this?

1. Put on your shoes so we can go.

   - (A) imperative
   - B declarative
   - C exclamatory
   - D interrogative

2. Where do you keep the bread?

   - A imperative
   - B declarative
   - C exclamatory
   - (D) interrogative

3. I am so happy to see you!

   - A imperative
   - B declarative
   - (C) exclamatory
   - D interrogative

4. I cook breakfast every Saturday.

   - A imperative
   - (B) declarative
   - C exclamatory
   - D interrogative

5. My sister poured the oil, and I added the egg.

   - A exclamatory
   - B interrogative
   - C simple
   - (D) compound

53

Working with Sentences

FRAGMENTS

You learned above that a sentence expresses a complete thought. A **fragment** is part of a sentence. It does not express a complete thought. It may be missing a subject, a verb, or both. A fragment cannot stand alone as a sentence. If you find a fragment in your writing, you will need to correct it to make it a complete sentence.

Example: Down the street.

This fragment leaves the reader asking questions. It is not a complete thought. To correct a fragment, add words to create a complete thought. This fragment does not have a subject or a verb, so they need to be added.

Possible correction:

The dog ran down the street.

FUNCTIONAL FRAGMENTS

There is one kind of fragment that can stand alone. It is called a **functional fragment**. Interjections like *Wow!* are examples. They are words or phrases that someone might shout without any other words around them. Also, words like *yes*, *no*, and *maybe* are common functional fragments. They serve a purpose even though they are not complete sentences.

Practice 3: Fragments

Which of these is a sentence fragment?

1.   A I missed the bus this morning.
       (B) Worked out for the best.
       C It started to snow.
       D School was dismissed early.

2.   A My dad arrived home soaking wet.
       B Apparently, he got splashed by a bus.
       (C) Especially without an umbrella.
       D He should have planned ahead!

Chapter 4

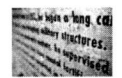

3   A   On Saturday, we are having a dinner party.
      B   We'll need to borrow some extra chairs.
      (C) If more than six people come over.
      D   My grandmother is making the dessert.

4   A   My best friend has a new baby sister.
      B   The baby is two weeks old.
      C   Mostly, she sleeps and cries all day.
      D   Just like my sister Annalise.

Which of these is a functional fragment?

5   A   Why?
     (B) Louie.
      C   What's?
      D   She said.

6 (A) Word around.
      B   Desk.
      C   Thinking.
      D   Help!

Working with Sentences

> **CHAPTER SUMMARY**
>
> A **subject** is who (or what) the sentence is about.
>
> A **predicate** tells something about the subject.
>
> Subjects and verbs must **agree**.
>
> A **simple sentence** has a subject and a verb.
>
> A **compound sentence** is two or more simple sentences joined by a comma and a word like *and*, *but*, or *so*.
>
> An **imperative** sentence gives a command.
>
> A **declarative** sentence makes a statement.
>
> An **exclamatory** sentence shows strong feeling and ends with an exclamation point.
>
> An **interrogative** sentence asks a question and ends with a question mark.
>
> A sentence **fragment** is part of a sentence. Sentence fragments need to be corrected. Some words and phrases, which are called **functional fragments**, can stand alone.

Chapter 4

CHAPTER 4 REVIEW

1. What is the subject of this sentence?

   Mandy sang in the chorus last year.

   (A) Mandy
   B   sang
   C   chorus
   D   last

2. What kind of sentence is this?

   I can bring brownies for the bake sale.

   A   imperative   (C) simple
   B   exclamatory   D   compound

3. What is the underlined part called?

   <u>Ouch!</u> Stop shooting those rubber bands at me!

   A   sentence fragment
   (B) functional fragment
   C   simple predicate
   D   complete subject

4. What is the simple predicate in this sentence?

   My babysitter played games with us.

   A   My babysitter
   B   babysitter
   (C) played
   D   played games with us

5. What kind of sentence is this?

   I think we should skate first and then go sledding.

   A   imperative   C   exclamatory
   (B) declarative   D   interrogative

57

Working with Sentences

6 Which sentence uses correct subject-verb agreement?

- A   Military planes often fly over my house.
- B   Military planes often flies over my house.
- C   Military planes often were fly over my house.
- D   Military planes often is flying over my house.

7 What kind of sentence is this?

| Can I bring money on the class trip? |

- A   imperative
- B   declarative
- C   exclamatory
- D   interrogative

8 Which sentence uses correct subject-verb agreement?

- A   A frog sit still to catch a bug.
- B   A frog is sits still to catch a bug.
- C   A frog sits still to catch a bug.
- D   A frog sitting still to catch a bug.

9 Which of these is a sentence fragment?

- A   Saw what happened.
- B   It was too late.
- C   We had played a trick.
- D   He laughed with us.

10 What is the complete subject of this sentence?

| After the game, the whole team went out for pizza. |

- A   game
- B   team
- C   the whole team
- D   the whole team went out

58

Chapter 5
Working with Paragraphs

This chapter covers the following Georgia CRCT standards and benchmarks:

ELA4W1: The student produces writing that establishes an appropriate organizational structure, sets a context and engages the reader, maintains a coherent focus throughout, and signals a satisfying closure. The student
a. Selects a focus, an organizational structure, and a point of view based on purpose, genre expectations, audience, length, and format requirements.
c. Uses traditional structures for conveying information (e.g., chronological order, cause and effect, similarity and difference, and posing and answering a question).
d. Uses appropriate structures to ensure coherence (e.g., transition elements).
ELA4W2: The student demonstrates competence in a variety of genres.
Nar e. Excludes extraneous details and inconsistencies.
Nar h. Provides a sense of closure to the writing.
Info d. Includes appropriate facts and details.
Info e. Excludes extraneous details and inappropriate information.
Info h. Provides a sense of closure to the writing.
Lit c. Supports judgments through references to the text, other works, authors, or non-print media, or references to personal knowledge.
Lit e. Excludes extraneous details and inappropriate information.
Lit f. Provides a sense of closure to the writing.
Per c. Supports a position with relevant evidence.
Per d. Excludes extraneous details and inappropriate information.
Per f. Provides a sense of closure to the writing.
ELA4W4: The student consistently uses a writing process to develop, revise, and evaluate writing. The student
b. Revises selected drafts to improve coherence and progression by adding, deleting, consolidating, and rearranging text.

You have learned about words and sentences. Now, it is time to use what you know to write paragraphs. A **paragraph** is a group of three to six sentences. These sentences all focus on one idea.

Working with Paragraphs

WHAT MAKES A GOOD PARAGRAPH?

Many things go into writing a good paragraph.

CONTENT

First, a paragraph must have good **content**. The whole paragraph should be about one topic. All of the sentences should talk about that topic.

Read the paragraph below.

> I am getting ready for the arrival of my new kitten. She is coming home next week, so I need many supplies. I bought a water bowl, a food dish, and a bag of cat food. I have a basket filled with kitty toys. I even set up a bed in the corner of my room. When my new kitten arrives next week, I will be prepared!

Notice how all of the sentences tell about the same thing. The main idea of the paragraph is to show how the writer has prepared for a new kitten. The writer sticks to the topic the whole way. Every sentence tells about the main idea. The reader has an easy time following the main idea.

Another thing to notice is how the writer tells about each idea just once. Ideas are not repeated. When you write, make sure you do not repeat the same idea over and over. You should **take out wording that is not related or repeats an idea**.

When you write a paragraph, think about content. Read over your own writing. Ask yourself:

- Is my main idea clear?
- Do all of my sentences tell about the main idea?
- Have I repeated any information?

STRUCTURE

Second, a paragraph must have good **structure**. A good paragraph has a beginning, a middle, and an end.

60

Chapter 5

A **topic sentence** comes at the beginning of a paragraph. A topic sentence tells the main idea of the paragraph. It is usually the first sentence.

The topic sentence from the paragraph above is "I am getting ready for the arrival of my new kitten."

A good opening sentence gets the reader's attention and clearly states the point of the paragraph.

Supporting sentences come in the middle of a paragraph. Supporting sentences tell more about the main idea.

Here are the supporting sentences from the paragraph above:

> She is coming home next week, so I need many supplies.
>
> I bought a water bowl, a food dish, and a bag of cat food.
>
> I have a basket filled with kitty toys.
>
> I set up a bed in the corner of my room.

Each supporting sentence relates to the topic sentence. The **order** of the supporting sentences should make sense too.

A **closing sentence** comes at the end of a paragraph. The closing sentence tells the main idea again, but in a different way.

The closing sentence from the paragraph above is "When my new kitten arrives next week, I will be prepared!"

A good closing sentence wraps up the discussion.

When you write a paragraph, think about structure. Read over your own writing. Ask yourself:

- Does my paragraph have a topic sentence at the beginning?
- Does my paragraph have supporting paragraphs in the middle?
- Does my paragraph have a concluding sentence at the end?
- Do all of my sentences make sense in the order they are in?

Working with Paragraphs

Practice 1: What Makes a Good Paragraph?

1 Which sentence would be the BEST to add to this paragraph?

> Valentine's Day parties in my class are a lot of fun. We get to bring a shoebox from home and decorate it during lesson time. After that, we deliver our valentines. Valentine's Day parties are a fun break from regular school.

A We listen to music while we open the valentines we got and eat cookies or cupcakes.

B Sometimes the principal stops by and tells us we are making too much noise.

C We have to make up all of our work at home that night.

D It takes a long time to make cards for everybody in the whole class.

2 Which sentence would BEST support the information in the paragraph?

> Sharks are often misunderstood. Many people think of sharks as dangerous. In fact, shark attacks on people are rare. To a shark, a surfer can look like a seal, which is a common food for a shark. People should stop thinking that sharks are out to get them.

A Sharks live for about twenty years.

B Shark attacks can happen when a shark mistakes a person for a fish.

C Sharks have teeth and fins.

D Sharks are not mammals, so they do not come to the surface for air.

Chapter 5

3 **Which sentence is unrelated to the paragraph?**

¹Last summer I had a great time at gymnastics camp. ²Each morning, we did tumbling and the balance beam. ³Our coaches had games for us to play during both events. ⁴After lunch we went swimming. ⁵Then we went back to the gym to do the bars and vault. ⁶Two people got sick. ⁷Our coaches had contests and prizes to win each day. ⁸We stayed up late watching movies and playing video games, and then got up for more gymnastics in the morning. ⁹Every day was fun from start to finish!

A   sentence 4
(B) sentence 6
C   sentence 8
D   sentence 9

4 **Which sentence repeats an idea in the paragraph?**

My little brother makes big messes. He is only three, so he can be clumsy. Last week, he spilled glue on the carpet. This morning, he knocked his cereal bowl on the floor, and milk went everywhere! He even spilled glue on the carpet one time. We all have to watch my brother closely and be ready for spills.

A   He is only three, so he can be clumsy.
B   This morning, he knocked his cereal bowl on the floor, and milk went everywhere!
(C) He even spilled glue on the carpet one time.
D   My little brother makes big messes.

5 **What is the BEST closing sentence for the paragraph?**

Being a firefighter is dangerous. A firefighter has to be brave enough to walk into a burning building. Climbing tall ladders, breathing in smoke, and rescuing people are all parts of the day's work.

A   My grandpa used to be a firefighter.
B   Firefighters wear a lot of gear.
C   Firefighters cook and sleep in the fire station.
(D) Firefighters face danger every day to help other people.

Working with Paragraphs

6 Which sentence should change places for the BEST clarity in the paragraph?

> ¹Instead of regular classes, we learn about different things. ²This week at school we are having a special event called "short term." ³We can take basket weaving, write for the newspaper, practice archery, and learn first aid. ⁴Short term gives us a chance to learn new things. ⁵It gives our teachers a chance to teach us about things they enjoy doing. ⁶Short term is like an in-school vacation for everyone.

A sentences 1 and 2
B sentences 2 and 3
C sentences 3 and 4
D sentences 4 and 5

WAYS TO ORGANIZE PARAGRAPHS

You read earlier that paragraphs must have good structure. Part of having good structure comes from organizing your ideas. There are different ways to organize a paragraph. These are called **organizational patterns**. They include chronological order, cause and effect, similarity and difference, or question and answer.

Chronological order is the order in which things happen. A paragraph that uses chronological order tells about events in the order that they happened. The paragraph below uses chronological order.

> When I get home from school each day, I have a routine I like to follow. First, I go to the kitchen and get a snack. I eat my snack outside while I play with my dog, Sophie. Then, I go inside and do my homework at the kitchen table while my dad prepares dinner. My dad and I talk when I'm done with my work. Finally, the rest of the family comes home.

A good paragraph often uses **transitions**. These are words or phrases that show connections between ideas. They help make writing smooth. They can also help make it easier to understand.

Chapter 5

Transitions in Chronological Paragraphs: You read above that chronological paragraphs tell things in the order that they happened. Transitionals in chronological paragraphs show time. *Finally, later on, meanwhile, next, then, today, soon,* and *when* are transitions often used in chronological paragraphs.

Cause and effect paragraphs tell what happens and why it happens. A cause and effect paragraph might tell mostly about why something happened (the cause). A cause and effect paragraph might tell mostly about the result of something happening (the effect). The paragraph below uses cause and effect.

> Many people are moving to my town. A new factory opened here last month. As a result, many people have moved here to work. Houses are inexpensive in my town. We also have friendly people and a great community center. Due to all of these things, people want to live in my town.

Transitions in Cause and Effect Paragraphs: Transition words for cause and effect paragraphs show relationships. *As a result, because of, due to,* and *so that* are transition words often used in cause and effect paragraphs.

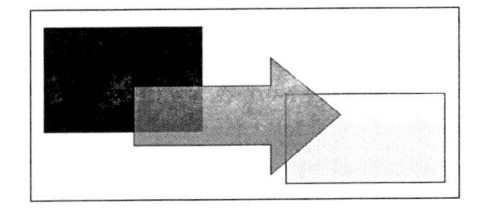

A **similarity and difference** (also called compare and contrast) paragraph tells how things are alike and how they are different. When you tell how things are similar, you are telling how things are alike. When you tell how things are different, you are discussing their differences. The paragraph below uses similarity and difference.

> Alligators and crocodiles are different in many ways. To begin with, their snouts are different shapes. An alligator has a wide snout, while a crocodile has a pointier snout. Alligators usually live in fresh water, but crocodiles usually live in salt water. Even though these two animals look similar, they are actually different animals.

Transitions in Similarity and Difference Paragraphs: Transitions for these paragraphs show how things are alike (compare) and different (contrast). *Just as, like, in addition,* and *similarly* are transitions often used to compare. *But, even though, however, instead of, otherwise, unlike,* and *while* are transitions used to contrast.

Working with Paragraphs

A **question and answer** paragraph asks a question and then answers it. A question and answer paragraph can also state a problem and then suggest solutions. The paragraph below uses this pattern.

> My sister and I watch the news. We feel terrible about the earthquake in Haiti. How can we help people in Haiti? It turns out that we have thought of a few ways. One thing we will do is have a yard sale. We will also put aside part of our allowances. We will send this money to one of the groups helping Haiti. As a result, we will be able to donate money we earn and save to help people there.

Transitions in Question and Answer Paragraphs: Transitions for question and answer paragraphs show results and explanations. *As a result, in fact, it turns out,* and *this is why* are some transitions that can be used in question and answer paragraphs.

As you can see, there are several ways to organize paragraphs. The structure you choose depends on your topic and your purpose for writing.

Practice 2: Ways to Organize Paragraphs

1. What kind of organization does the paragraph use?

> ¹This year, I went with my family to Sarasota, Florida for spring break. ²I had a lot of fun the first day collecting shells on the beach. ³That evening, we ate dinner at a restaurant on the beach. ⁴The next morning, we went to a circus museum, and then rode bicycles at a state park. ⁵Each day in Sarasota was an adventure.

    A   chronological order
    B   cause and effect
    C   similarity and difference
    D   question and answer

Chapter 5

2 What kind of organization does the paragraph use?

> ¹Riding a skateboard without pads is dangerous. ²There are many ways to get hurt if you don't wear proper protection. ³If put out your hand to break your fall, you can break your wrist if you are not wearing wristguards. ⁴If you land on your knees without kneepads, you can skin your knee. ⁵Due to the danger of skateboarding, it is smart to wear the right equipment.

- A chronological order
- (B) cause and effect
- C similarity and difference
- D question and answer

3 What kind of organization does the paragraph use?

> ¹There are several reasons that I choose not to eat candy. ²First of all, candy sticks in my braces. ³I have had three cavities, and getting them filled is not fun. ⁴Third, when I eat more than one piece of candy, I often start to feel sick. ⁵For those reasons, I have decided to stop eating candy.

- (A) chronological order
- B cause and effect
- C similarity and difference
- D question and answer

4 Which transition would BEST connect sentences 2 and 3?

- (A) Second,
- B Last,
- C However,
- D While

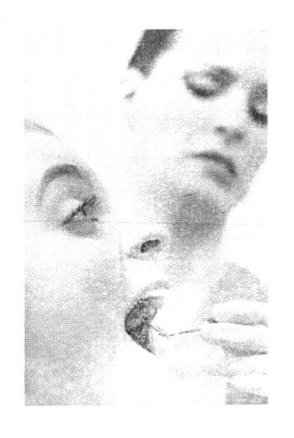

67

Working with Paragraphs

5 What kind of organization does the paragraph use?

> ¹My pets, a snake and a dog, are very different from each other. ²My dog is cuddly; my snake is not. ³My dog needs a lot of exercise. ⁴My snake spends a lot of the day sleeping. ⁵My dog likes to be around people, while my snake prefers to be left alone. ⁶I love both of my pets, but they are very different animals.

- A chronological order
- B cause and effect
- **C similarity and difference**
- D question and answer

6 Which transition would BEST connect sentences 3 and 4?

- A In contrast,
- B Likewise,
- C So,
- **D In addition,**

7 What kind of organization does the paragraph use?

> ¹Many people are wondering how to get kids to be more active. ²One solution would be to have more community centers. ³I would play basketball every day if I could walk to a community center near my house. ⁴I think it would help to have a contest at school to see who got the most exercise each week. ⁵A contest might encourage kids to try harder.

- A chronological order
- B cause and effect
- C similarity and difference
- **D question and answer**

8 Which transition would BEST connect sentences 3 and 4?

- **A As a result,**
- B Also,
- C Since
- D Like

Chapter 5

9 What kind of organization does the paragraph use?

> ¹Have you ever watched what a dog does before going to sleep? ²My dog has a certain things she does before every nap. ³First, she turns around in a circle two times. ⁴Then, she flops down and groans. ⁵Finally, she nuzzles her head into a comfortable position. ⁶She drops off to sleep.

- A chronological order
- B cause and effect
- C similarity and difference
- D question and answer

10 Which transition would BEST connect sentences 5 and 6?

- A In fact,
- B First,
- C But,
- D At last,

MORE ABOUT TRANSITIONS

In addition to within paragraphs, there are a few other ways to use transitions.

TRANSITIONS BETWEEN PARAGRAPHS

Besides connecting ideas in sentences, transitions also connect ideas between paragraphs. Transitions show how ideas are related. They help a reader follow ideas from one paragraph to the next.

Example:

There are many people who think it is a good idea to have separate classes for boys and girls. Some studies show that girls do better in certain subjects, like math, if there are only girls in the class. Other studies show that boys focus more on their work when there are only boys in the class.

Even though there are studies to support separating girls from boys, many people think the opposite. These people think that it is not natural to separate boys and girls. They think that boys and girls are together in the real world, so they need to learn to get along in the classroom.

Working with Paragraphs

Notice how the first sentence of the second paragraph relates to ideas in the first paragraph. It uses a transition phrase (*even though*). This shows it will talk about a contrasting idea. This is one way to connect ideas between paragraphs. You can also use other transitions to show how ideas relate.

As you see, to tie paragraphs together, you can repeat some key words. It also helps to use transition words and phrases. These are the same ones that are used within paragraphs.

TRANSITIONAL STRUCTURES

Transitions also help break down writing into parts. This can make writing easier to understand. It can also help readers know what to expect. In an outline, you can use **numbers** and **subheadings** to do this. An **outline** shows a plan of what you will cover when you write. Below is the structure an outline uses.

Topic

I. Point 1 (Heading)

    A. First subpoint for Point 1 (Subheading)

    B. Second subpoint for Point 1 (Subheading)

II. Point 2 (Heading)

    A. First subpoint for Point 2 (Subheading)

    B. Second subpoint for Point 2 (Subheading)

Here is an outline that has been filled in. Notice how the outline is numbered and uses headings and subheadings.

Important People in My Life

I. Family

    A. My sister

    B. My parents

II. Friends

    A. Jesse

    B. William

Chapter 5

After reading this outline, you know the main things the writer will discuss. Breaking the ideas down shows the main points and how they are related.

You can use your outline to write paragraphs. When you do, be sure to change the numbers and subheadings to transition words or phrases. Look at this example. The transitions are underlined.

Outline form

II. Friends

    A. Jesse

    B. William

Paragraph form

<u>Just like</u> my family, my friends are very important to me. My best friend is Jesse. <u>First</u>, he and I grew up a few houses apart. Our parents <u>also</u> are great friends. <u>Another</u> good friend of mine is William. I have not known him as long, <u>but</u> he is a really good friend <u>too</u>. We play baseball together. <u>In addition</u>, he's really smart and helps me study.

Another way to show how ideas are related is to use **bullets**. You can use bullets with a list of items. Bullets break down a big thing into smaller parts. Each smaller part is equal. The items are not in a special order.

    Example: Things to do on Saturday

- Clean the garage
- Wash the dog
- Work on social studies project
- Vacuum the car

Working with Paragraphs

Practice 3: More about Transitions

Read the outline below. Then answer the two questions that follow.

Kinds of Pets

I. Guinea pig

   A. What you can do with it

   B. Amount of work

II. Dog

   A. What you can do with it

   B̶. Amount of work

III. lizard

   A. What you can do with it

   B. Amount of work

1 Which letter or number would BEST complete the outline?

   (A) B   C III
   B A   D C

2 Which heading would BEST complete the outline?

   A elephant   C houseplant
   (B) lizard   D grandma

3 Which item would BEST complete the bulleted list?

Before leaving for school each morning

- Pack lunch
- Pack snack
- Make bed

   (A) Paint house   C Leave for vacation
   B Play with friends   D Brush teeth

Chapter 5

4 **Which transitional sentence BEST connects the two paragraphs?**

> Playing soccer is great exercise. There are few breaks during a soccer game, which means that players run for most of the game. Soccer is a good workout for the whole body.
>
> _____ Soccer players often hurt their knees. My best friend knocked out both of her front teeth playing soccer, and my cousin's teammate broke his arm. Because soccer is a tiring sport, it is important to stay aware of what is happening on the field in order to stay safe.

A   Soccer players make a lot of money and can even be famous.
B   Soccer jerseys come in many colors; my favorite is green.
C   Soccer is good exercise, but is hard on the body.
D   Soccer is too dangerous to play very often.

5 **Which transitional sentence BEST connects the two paragraphs?**

> Cooking can be both fun and educational. When you cook, you get to be creative. You can follow a recipe or even invent a new one. Cooking is an activity you can do with a friend. When my friend Sam comes over, we often bake brownies.
>
> _____ Cooking teaches you about math. You need to measure ingredients when you cook. Sometimes you will need to add fractions and divide. Cooking is a fun way to practice what I am learning in math.

A   Cooking is messy, so be prepared to clean up after yourself.
B   Another good thing about cooking is that it is educational.
C   One thing I really enjoy about cooking is tasting what I make.
D   Cooking can be dangerous if you are not careful.

Working with Paragraphs

> **CHAPTER SUMMARY**
>
> All sentences in a **paragraph** should be about one topic.
>
> A paragraph should start with a **topic sentence. Supporting sentences** come next, followed by the **closing sentence**.
>
> Paragraphs can be **organized** in different ways. **Chronological, cause and effect, similarity and difference, question and answer** are all ways to organize paragraphs.
>
> Use **transitions** to connect ideas.

CHAPTER 5 REVIEW

1 Which sentence would BEST support the information in the paragraph?

> Making a balloon animal is harder than it looks. You need to leave some room at the end of the balloon for air to move around. If you put too much air in the balloon, it will pop when you try to twist it. It takes practice to know how to handle a balloon when you are trying to shape it into an animal.

   (A) Sections of the balloon may pop while you are twisting.
   B   Balloons come in many different colors and shapes.
   C   Balloons are made of rubber and are dangerous for babies.
   D   Some balloons are filled with helium.

Chapter 5

2 **Which sentence is unrelated to the paragraph?**

> If you like reading about the wilderness, you would probably enjoy the book *Hatchet*. It is about a boy named Brian. His plane crashes deep in the woods. The story tells how Brian survives alone in the woods for a long time. Plane crashes are fairly rare events. We see what Brian eats and where he sleeps. We also see how Brian deals with problems. The book is about different kinds of survival.

- A We see what Brian eats and where he sleeps.
- B Plane crashes are fairly rare events.
- C We also see how Brian deals with problems.
- D The story tells how Brian survives alone in the woods for a long time.

3 **Which sentence repeats an idea in the paragraph?**

> Getting enough sleep is important. When people do not sleep enough, they can be grouchy. Being tired can keep people from thinking clearly. Studies have even shown that drivers have more accidents when they are tired. Tired people can be grouchy at times. Everyone needs to get enough sleep.

- A Studies have even shown that drivers have more accidents when they are tired.
- B Tired people can be grouchy at times.
- C Getting enough sleep is important.
- D Being tired can keep people from thinking clearly.

4 **What is the BEST closing sentence for the paragraph?**

> Swimming is a sport that nearly anyone can do. Babies and young children enjoy splashing in pools and at the beach. Many kids join a swim team in the summer. Many adults swim for both exercise and fun. Even people who have injuries can do it. In fact, when it is hard to walk, they can move more easily in water.

- A Swimming is not a difficult skill to learn.
- B People who swim often have strong arms and legs.
- C Some people may be afraid of the water.
- D Swimming is something people can do their whole lives.

Working with Paragraphs

5 Which sentence would be the BEST to add to this paragraph?

> My favorite season is fall. I love seeing the leaves change color. The cooler air is pleasant after the hot summer. Fall always means a trip to the pumpkin farm with my family. I always look forward to fall.

- A I wish we had school in the summer rather than in the fall.
- B Summer is my favorite time to go on vacation.
- C Fall means apple picking for me and baking for my mom.
- D Sometimes I think it is too cold in the fall.

6 What kind of organization does the paragraph use?

> ¹Everyone says my sister and I are alike. ²We both love salty snacks, but we don't like chocolate. ³We both like to talk on the phone. ⁴I enjoy playing basketball, and so does my sister. ⁵I would rather stay up late than get up early. ⁶Everyone says we are "two peas in a pod."

- A chronological order
- B cause and effect
- C similarity and difference
- D question and answer

7 Which transition would BEST connect sentences 4 and 5?

- A Without my sister,
- B Like my sister,
- C Instead of my sister,
- D Because of my sister,

Chapter 5

8 What kind of organization does the paragraph use?

> ¹When making a bed, there are certain steps to follow. ²First, put on the fitted sheet. ³Put on the flat sheet. ⁴Top this with a blanket and a quilt. ⁵Then put the pillowcases on the pillows. ⁶Now your bed is ready to sleep in.

- (A) chronological order
- B cause and effect
- C similarity and difference
- D question and answer

9 Which transition would BEST connect sentences 2 and 3?

- A Finally,
- (B) Next,
- C First,
- D So,

10 What kind of organization does the paragraph use?

> ¹Saving money helps me get the things I really want. ²When I was younger, I used to spend my money as soon as I got it. ³I wasted money on cheap things that broke quickly. ⁴Now that I am older, I spend more carefully. ⁵I can afford to buy things that cost more and are nicer. ⁶Recently, I saved enough to buy a pair of sneakers that I really wanted.

- A chronological order
- (B) cause and effect
- C similarity and difference
- D question and answer

77

Working with Paragraphs

Read the outline below. Then answer the two questions that follow.

Should I Visit the Beach or the Pool?

I. Beach

    A. Can build castles

    __. Can look for shells

    C. Can climb on the rocks

II. Pool

    A. _____

    B. Can float on the raft

    C. Can use the dive toys

11 Which letter or number would BEST complete the outline?

    A B
    B A
    C III
    D C

12 Which subheading would BEST complete the outline for II.A?

    A Can bury myself in sand
    B Can go fishing
    C Can fly a kite
    D Can practice diving

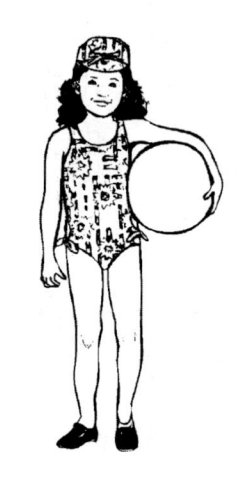

Chapter 6
Kinds of Writing

This chapter covers the following Georgia CRCT standard and benchmarks:

ELAW4: The student consistently uses a writing process to develop, revise, and evaluate writing. The student
a. Plans and drafts independently and resourcefully.
c. Edits to correct errors in spelling, punctuation, etc.

When you write, what do you do first? Do you pick a topic right away? Do you make a list of all the things you'd like to write about? Different people approach writing in different ways. But, one thing is true for everyone. Good writing starts with a plan.

TYPES OF WRITING

One thing to consider is what type of writing you will use. There are many kinds. Each is a little different. Your approach to writing depends on what you will write about.

Some common types of writing are listed here. As you can see, each type of writing has a different purpose.

Narrative writing	tells a story. It could be an essay about a hero. It might be a story about a time you helped a friend. These are just two examples.
Informational writing	describes a process or teaches about a topic. One example is the manual that comes with a video-game system. Another is a brochure about a museum. Chapters in textbooks also are examples.
Response to literature	is thoughtful writing a student does after reading a story, book, or poem. For example, your teacher may ask you to compare characters in *Harriet the Spy*. Or, you might write about how you felt after reading a poem.
Persuasive writing	tells the writer's view on an issue. The writer tries to convince the reader to agree. One example is a letter to the editor in a newspaper that tells the writer's opinion about the war in Afghanistan.

No matter what type of writing you are doing, having a plan helps you get started. It is like a road map to get you where you want to go!

Kinds of Writing

THE WRITING PROCESS

When you plan, you think about how you will write. You consider what you want to say. You also decide how to organize your essay. You think about what is important to include.

Part of planning is using a series of steps to get started. This is called the **writing process**. The steps break the big task (writing an essay) into smaller parts. Here are the steps:

- Prewriting
- Drafting
- Revising
- Editing
- Publishing

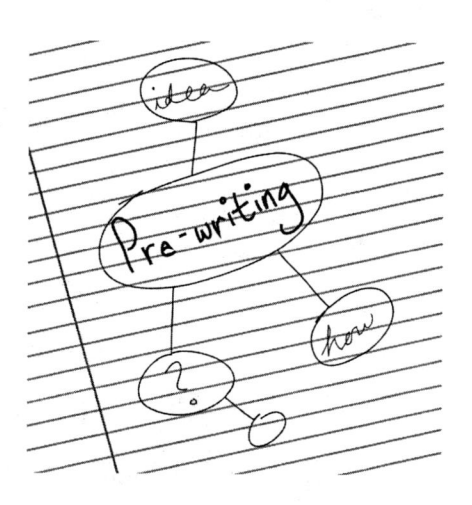

PREWRITING

The first step in the writing process is **prewriting**. This is when you do most of your planning. During prewriting, you will choose a topic. You think about how to organize your thoughts. You might do research or make lists.

> **Example:**
>
> Tia is writing an essay for her language arts class. The assignment is to compare two characters in *Charlie and the Chocolate Factory* by Roald Dahl.

The first thing Tia does is plan. She needs to figure out what kind of writing to do. She decides that this essay will be a response to literature. Tia knows that, in this type of writing, she needs to answer a question about what she has read. In this case, her task is to tell about two characters. She knows that she will use examples from the book to support her ideas.

80

Next, Tia needs to decide which characters to use. She starts by making a list of the characters she might choose.

Charlie Bucket	Mike Teavee
Charlie's mom	Violet Beauregarde
Grandpa Joe	Augustus Gloop
Veruca Salt	Mr. Wonka

Tia considers each choice. She decides that she will use Charlie Bucket and Veruca Salt. They are both kids who find a golden ticket. But they are very different from each other. She decides she will talk about how they differ from each other. She crosses out the other names on her list.

Tia then makes a list. She has one column for Charlie and one for Veruca. She lists all the ways in which the two are different.

<u>Charlie</u>	<u>Veruca</u>
obedient	greedy
kind	disobedient
thoughtful	selfish
poor	spoiled
respectful	rich
	demanding

Now Tia has a plan. She has a good idea of what she will write about. She is ready for the next step in the writing process. Keep reading to see how Tia follows the steps of the writing process.

DRAFTING

After you prewrite, it is time to draft. **Drafting** is the second step in the writing process. This is the step when you start to organize your ideas. You start to work on paragraphs. What should you include in these paragraphs? It depends on what you are writing.

Kinds of Writing

CHOOSING A FOCUS

As you draft, you will begin to **focus** your writing. Keeping the focus in mind will help you decide how to approach your writing.

Narrative writing	focuses on entertaining the reader by telling a story. When you write, tell about characters, plot, and setting.
Informational writing	focuses on informing. It can show a process. It can teach about a topic. When you write, include specific facts and details.
Response to literature	focuses on reflecting on what you've read. When you write, focus on your thoughts about what you have read and what it means to you.
Persuasive writing	focuses on trying to get others to agree with you. In persuasive writing, it is important to make a claim and support it.

As you can see, the focus can change. It depends on what type of writing you choose. The right focus will help you decide what to include and what words to use. Knowing your focus will help you decide if you should include your opinion, or just stick to the facts.

You read in chapter 5 about paragraphs. Use the rules for writing good paragraphs to draft your essay. Each one should start with a topic sentence, have supporting details, and end with a concluding sentence. All of the sentences should be about the same topic. (For more about paragraphs, review chapter 5.)

Example:

When Tia begins her draft, she thinks about her focus. She knows that she is doing a response to literature. So, her focus should be on answering the question about the book she read. She has already decided to talk about Charlie and Veruca. Now, she takes her prewriting and uses it to draft an essay.

Chapter 6

Here is what Tia writes:

> Charlie and Veruca are two characters in Charlie and the chocolate factory. That is the only thing they have in commen. These two people are very different.
>
> Charlie offers too share his chocolate with his grandparents. Even though he hardly ever gets chocolate. Veruca is selfish. She screams until her dad gets her a ticket.
>
> Charlie is obedient. Example, in the field before they get on the boat, Charlie listens and follows directions. Veruca is greedy. She yells to get what she wants. She cares most about getting her way.
>
> In the end, Charlie wins. The whiole time in the Factory, he was being respectful and kind. Veruca gets into trouble. She ends up falling down garbage chute because she is greedy. She loses mr wonka's contest. Charlie wins.
>
> If I could choose, Charlie is who I would want for a Friend. He is generous, thoughtful and kind. It is no wonder Mr Wonka hooped that Charlie would win. Veruca is greedy and selfish.

This is Tia's first draft. Notice that it is messy. There are spelling errors and grammar errors. That is OK. These things are not important in a first draft. The important part of this step is to get your thoughts on paper. You will correct these errors later.

Kinds of Writing

Practice 1: Planning Your Writing

Read the information below. Then, answer the questions that follow.

You have been given the following essay topic:

"Describe how to shoot a basket."

1. What type of essay should you write for this topic?

   A   narrative
   B   informational
   C   persuasive
   D   response to literature

2. Which would be the BEST focus for this essay?

   A   the steps to shooting a basket
   B   favorite sports of fourth graders
   C   where people like to play ball
   D   how to win a basketball game

3. You are prewriting about the best things about going to camp. What would be the BEST thing to add to your list?

   Best parts of camp

   swimming

   archery

   canoeing

   camping in a tent

   _____

   A   mosquitoes
   B   sunburn
   C   horseback riding
   D   early bedtime

Chapter 6

You are writing a persuasive essay that says girls should be allowed to play football.

4 What information would be BEST to include in this type of essay?

   A   information about your favorite football player
   B   a funny story about the time you went to football camp
   C   reasons you think girls should be able to play football
   D   details about how the game of football is played

5 In which step of the writing process should you start organizing your ideas into paragraphs?

   A   prewriting
   B   drafting
   C   revising
   D   editing

REVISING YOUR WRITING

The third step of the writing process is **revising**. Revising means making changes to improve your work. First, you re-read your work. Then, you do things like add details. You might rearrange some sentences or even paragraphs. You can get others to read your work and give you reactions. You could ask friends in your class or the teacher.

Here are some questions you might ask when revising:

- Do my ideas make sense in the order they are in?
- Is there anything that doesn't make sense?
- Does each paragraph have a main idea?
- Do I have good supporting sentences?
- Did I repeat anything?
- Can I add any details?
- Do I need to add any transitions?

Kinds of Writing

Tia reads over her draft. She asks herself the questions above. She is looking for "big" issues. These include organization, supporting details, and repeated ideas. Tia will make the smaller corrections later.

Here is how Tia revises her essay:

> Charlie and Veruca are two characters in Charlie and the chocolate factory by Roald Dahl. While both are children invited to tour the factory, this is the only thing they have in commen. These two people are very different. They do not have much in commen.
>
> One example of this is at the beginning of the book when Charlie offers too share his chocolate with his grandparents. Even though he hardly ever gets chocolate. Veruca, on the other hand, is selfish from the start. She screams until her dad gets her a ticket.
>
> Charlie is an obedient child. At the start of the factory tour, everyone is in a field before boarding the boat. In this scene, Charlie listens and follows directions, while Veruca is greedy and disobedient. She yells to get what she wants. Veruca cares most about getting her way.
>
> In the end, Charlie wins Mr. Wonka's contest. The whiole time in the Factory, he was being respectful and kind. Veruca gets into trouble. She ends up falling down a garbage chute because she is greedy. So, she loses mr wonkas contest. Charlie wins.
>
> If I could choose, Charlie is who I would want for a Friend. He is generous, thoughtful and kind. It is no wonder Mr Wonka hooped that Charlie would win. Veruca is greedy and selfish.

Notice the changes Tia made. In the first paragraph, she added the name of the author. This is an important detail. She also added two ways that Charlie and Veruca are alike: they are both kids, and they both go to the chocolate factory. Adding this detail helps their many differences stand out.

Chapter 6

In the paragraphs 2 and 3, Tia adds examples from the book. This is important to do in a response to literature.

In the paragraph 3, Tia adds a detail. She explains what Charlie won (Mr. Wonka's contest). She has also added some transitions like *on the other hand*, *while*, and *so* to help her ideas flow.

Now, it's your turn. Look for some more ways to improve Tia's essay.

Practice 2: Revising Your Writing

Read the paragraphs from Tia's draft. Then answer the questions that follow.

1 Which sentence should be deleted because it repeats an idea?

> [1]Charlie and Veruca are two characters in Charlie and the chocolate factory. [2]While both are children invited to tour the factory, this is the only thing they have in commen. [3]These two people are very different. [4]They do not have much in commen.

    A   sentence 1
    B   sentence 2
    C   sentence 3
    D   sentence 4

2 Which sentence would be the BEST to start this paragraph?

> One example of this is at the beginning of the book when he offers too share his chocolate with his grandparents. Even though he hardly ever gets chocolate. Veruca, on the other hand is selfish from the start. She screams until her dad gets her a ticket.

    A   Charlie is generous.
    B   Charlie is not perfect.
    C   Charlie is selfish.
    D   Charlie is rich.

Kinds of Writing

3 Which sentence would BEST support the information in the paragraph?

> Charlie is an obedient child. At the start of the factory tour, everyone is in a field before boarding the boat. In this scene, Charlie listens and follows directions while Veruca is greedy and disobedient. She yells to get what she wants. Veruca cares most about getting her way.

A   She rows the boat herself.
B   She demands that her father buy whatever she sees.
C   She shakes Mr. Wonka's hand.
D   She offers some candy to the other children on the tour.

4 What is the BEST way to add a transition to sentence 3?

> ¹In the end, Charlie wins Mr. Wonka's contest. ²The whiole time in the Factory, he was being respectful and kind. ³Veruca gets into trouble. ⁴She ends up falling down a garbage chute because she is greedy, so she loses mr wonkas contest. ⁵Charlie wins.

A   In addition, Veruca gets into trouble.
B   Likewise, Veruca gets into trouble.
C   However, Veruca gets into trouble.
D   First, Veruca gets into trouble.

5 Which sentences should change places?

> ¹If I could choose, Charlie is who I would want for a Friend. ²He is generous, thoughtful and kind. ³It is no wonder Mr Wonka hooped that Charlie would win. ⁴Veruca is greedy and selfish.

A   sentences 1 and 4
B   sentences 2 and 4
C   sentences 1 and 2
D   sentences 3 and 4

Chapter 6

EDITING YOUR WRITING

The fourth step in the writing process is **editing**. When you edit, you look for small errors. These include spelling and punctuation. You use what you know about grammar and mechanics to make your writing clear and correct.

Now, Tia is at the editing step. She reads her work for details. She pays attention to things like spelling, sentence fragments, and punctuation. (For more about what to look for, review chapters 1 through 4 in this book.) Help Tia edit her work in Practice 3.

Planning

Drafting

Revising

★ Editing

Practice 3: Editing Your Writing

Read what Tia has written. Then, answer the questions that follow.

1 **Which word is misspelled in this sentence?**

> While both are children invited to tour the factory, this is the only thing they have in commen.

A   children
B   invited
C   factory
D   commen

2 **Which part of the paragraph is a sentence fragment?**

> ¹One example of this is at the beginning of the book when he offers too share his chocolate with his grandparents. ²Even though he hardly ever gets chocolate. ³Veruca, on the other hand is selfish from the start. ⁴She screams until her dad gets her a ticket.

A   sentence 1
B   sentence 2
C   sentence 3
D   sentence 4

Kinds of Writing

3 Which choice corrects the errors in this sentence?

> So, she loses mr wonkas contest.

- A So, she loses mr wonka's contest.
- B So, she loses mr. Wonkas contest.
- C So, she loses Mr. Wonkas contest.
- (D) So, she loses Mr. Wonka's contest.

4 Which choice corrects the comma error in this sentence?

> He is generous, thoughtful and kind.

- A He is generous thoughtful, and kind.
- B He is generous, thoughtful and, kind.
- (C) He is generous, thoughtful, and kind.
- D He is, generous thoughtful and kind.

5 Which sentence in the paragraph contains errors in capitalization and spelling?

> [1]In the end, Charlie wins Mr. Wonka's contest. [2]The whiole time in the Factory, he was being respectful and kind. [3]Veruca got into trouble. [4]She ends up falling down a garbage chute because she is greedy.

- A sentence 1   C sentence 3
- (B) sentence 2   D sentence 4

PUBLISHING

The final step in the writing process is publishing. When you **publish** your writing, you share the final version with others. You might read your essay aloud to your class. Your teacher might hang your essay on the wall. You might print it off to hand in. Or, you could post it to an online site for your class. When you share the finished copy in these ways, you are publishing.

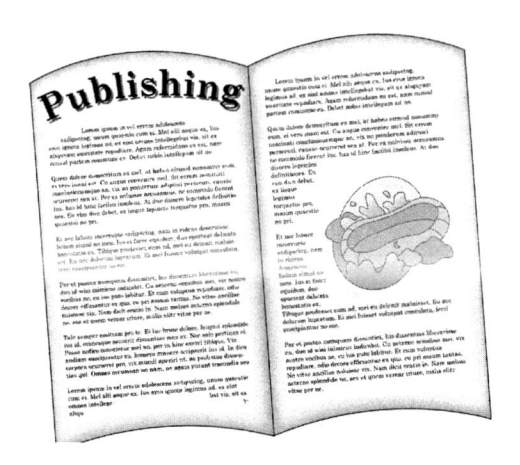

Chapter 6

Here is Tia's final draft. It is ready to publish.

Charlie and Veruca: Two Very Different Kids in the Chocolate Factory

Charlie and Veruca are two characters in *Charlie and the Chocolate Factory* by Roald Dahl. While both are children invited to tour the factory, this is the only thing they have in common. These two characters are very different.

Charlie is generous. One example of this is at the beginning of the book when he offers to share his chocolate with his grandparents, even though he hardly ever gets chocolate. Veruca, on the other hand, is selfish from the start. She screams until her dad gets her a golden ticket.

Charlie is an obedient child. At the start of the factory tour, everyone is in a field before boarding the boiled sweet boat. In this scene, Charlie listens and follows directions, while Veruca is greedy and disobedient. She demands that her father buy whatever she sees. She yells to get what she wants. It is clear that Veruca cares most about getting her way.

In the end, Charlie wins Mr. Wonka's contest. The whole time in the factory, he was respectful and kind. However, Veruca got into trouble. She ended up falling down a garbage chute because she was greedy. So, she loses Mr. Wonka's contest. Charlie wins.

If I could choose, Charlie is who I would want for a friend. He is generous, thoughtful, and kind. Veruca is greedy and selfish. It is no wonder Mr. Wonka hoped that Charlie would win.

Kinds of Writing

CHAPTER SUMMARY

Narrative writing tells a story.

Informational writing describes a process or teaches about a topic.

Response to literature is thoughtful writing a student does after reading a story or a poem.

Persuasive writing tells the writer's view on an issue.

Plan your writing to figure out how to start and what you want to say.

The steps in the **writing process** are prewrite, draft, revise, edit, and publish.

- **Prewriting** is your planning stage. You choose a topic and organize your thoughts.
- **Drafting** is the early step of organizing your thoughts into paragraphs.
- **Revising** means adding details and rearranging your writing.
- **Editing** is the important step of looking for small errors, like spelling and punctuation.
- **Publishing** is the final step, in which you share your writing with others.

Chapter 6 Review

Answer the questions that follow.

1. In which step of the writing process do you share your finished work with others?

    A   prewriting
    B   publishing
    C   editing
    D   revising

You have been given the following essay question:

> "Tell about the best birthday you have ever had."

2. What kind of essay should you write for this question?

    A   narrative
    B   informational
    C   persuasive
    D   genre

3. Which would be the BEST focus for this essay?

    A   Tell a story to entertain your reader.
    B   Teach about something you did.
    C   Share your response to a poem you read.
    D   Try to get others to agree with you.

4. When would you choose your focus?

    A   while drafting
    B   while revising
    C   while editing
    D   while publishing

Kinds of Writing

Use the paragraph below to answer questions 5 though 8.

> [1]Of all of my jobs, giving my dog, Ellie, a bath is the hardest. [2]Ellie does not like baths, so she hides when she sees what is happening. [3]Ellie is five years old; I got her when I was four. [4]When I finally get her into the backyard, I have to hold her leash and try to wash her at the same time. [5]She squirmes and tries to run. [6]Of course, she shakes the water off as often as possible, so I always end up wet too.

5 Which sentence is unrelated to the paragraph?

- A She squirmes and tries to run.
- B Ellie is five years old; I got her when I was four.
- C Of all of my jobs, giving my dog, Ellie, a bath is the hardest.
- D Ellie does not like baths, so she hides when sees what is happening.

6 When would you fix this error?

- A while prewriting
- B while drafting
- C while editing
- D while revising

7 Which sentence contains a spelling error?

- A sentence 2
- B sentence 3
- C sentence 4
- D sentence 5

8 When would you check your work for spelling errors?

- A while prewriting
- B while revising
- C while editing
- D while publishing

Chapter 7
Research

This chapter covers the following Georgia CRCT standard and benchmarks:

ELA4W3 The student uses research and technology to support writing. The student
a. Acknowledges information from sources.
b. Locates information in reference texts by using organizational features (i.e., prefaces, appendices, indices, glossaries, and tables of contents).
c. Uses various reference materials (i.e., dictionary, thesaurus, encyclopedia, electronic information, almanac, atlas, magazines, newspapers, and key words).
d. Demonstrates basic keyboarding skills and familiarity with computer terminology (e.g., software, memory, disk drive, hard drive).

Did you ever write a report? If so, you probably needed to look up some information. Did you know where to look to find what you needed? Was it easy to find? Knowing where to look makes it easier to use books and other sources.

ORGANIZATIONAL FEATURES

Many times, you will use books to look up facts. A book you use for research is often divided into parts. When you know about these parts, you can find what you need more easily.

PREFACE

A **preface** is a section that introduces the book. It tells the purpose of the book and what it covers. It may tell why the author wrote the book and how he got his information. A preface is found at the beginning of a book.

Example: Here is part of a preface from a book about spiders.

This book covers the life cycle of spiders. I wrote this book after my brother started keeping a spider for a pet. Thank you to my brother, Rob, and the helpful experts at the Spider Research Institute for their help.

Research

TABLE OF CONTENTS

A **table of contents** lists the parts of a book in order. It has the names of chapters and the pages they start on. A table of contents is found at the beginning of a book, after the preface.

Example: Here is part of a table of contents from a book about bears.

Chapter 1: Kinds of Bears	page 1
Chapter 2: Habitat	page 19
Chapter 3: Eating	page 25
Chapter 4: Hibernation	page 37

APPENDIX

An **appendix** is extra material at the end of a book. It can contain extra pieces like maps or charts. It might also give more places to explore about the topic.

Example: This book is about Georgia history. One chapter mentions the explorers. Then, this appendix entry gives more information.

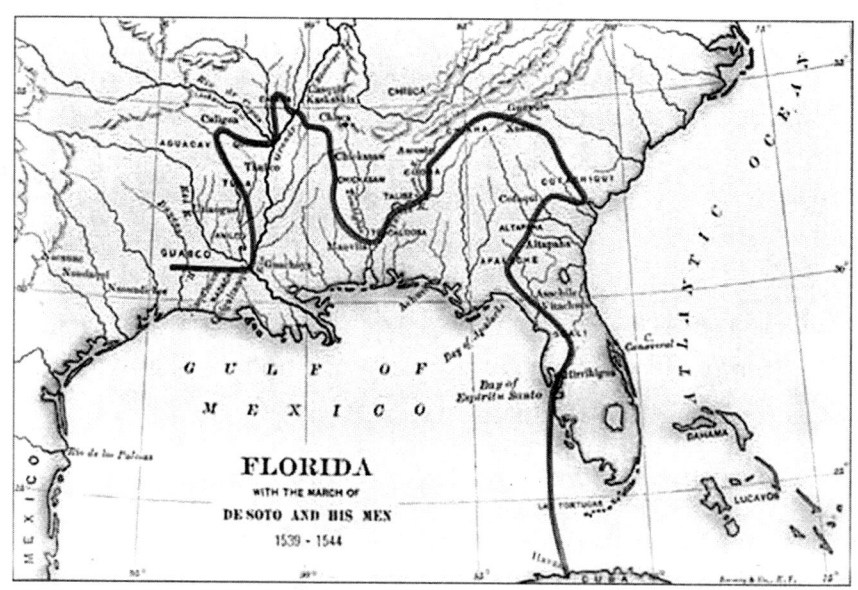

This map shows the route Hernando de Soto took through Georgia. You can see the parts of Georgia he passed through. Did he go near any place you have lived or visited?

96

Chapter 7

GLOSSARY

A **glossary** is a list of certain words used in the book. These words are ones the reader may not already know. A glossary is a section at the end of the book that tells the meaning of these words. It is like a mini dictionary.

> **Example:** This glossary might appear at the back of the book *A Field Guide to Wildflowers*. Notice that the entries are in alphabetical order.

> petal—the colored part of a flower
>
> sepal—a part of the flower that protects the bud
>
> stamen—the part of a flower where the pollen is

INDEX

An **index** is a list at the end of a book. It tells on which page you can find a topic or subject. An index is in alphabetical order.

> **Example:** This book tells about things to do around Atlanta. Here is part of the index.

> Animal farms 161
>
> Animal shelters 158–160
>
> Anna Ruby Falls 328
>
> Antebellum plantations 83

Practice 1: Organizational Features

Answer the questions below.

1. Which part of a book contains definitions of words used in the book?

    A preface   C appendix
    B glossary (circled) D table of contents

2. Which part of a book gives extra information about topics in the book?

    A preface   C appendix (circled)
    B glossary   D index

97

Research

3. Jennifer is using a book about farming in Georgia. She wants to know on which page pecan trees are found. Which feature should she use?

   A glossary
   B appendix
   C table of contents
   D index

4. Read the index below. On which page would you find information on peaches?

   > parsnips 67
   > peaches 68
   > plums 72
   > potatoes 73

   A 67
   B 68
   C 72
   D 73

5. When does it make more sense to use an index instead of a table of contents?

   A when you are looking for a specific topic
   B when you are looking for which page chapter 3 starts on
   C when you are looking for a definition of a word
   D when you are looking for the author of the book

   > "This book looks at how climate affected early life in Georgia. I thank the Georgia Historical Society for its generous help."

6. This is an example of a

   A preface.
   B glossary.
   C appendix.
   D index.

Chapter 7

USING SOURCES

Books are good sources of information. There are other sources you can use too. The best source to use often depends on what you want to know. If you wanted to see the path the Chattahoochee River follows, you would use one kind of source. If you wanted to learn about the planet Mars, you would use a different kind of source. The table below shows different kinds of sources.

Types of Sources		
Source	Description	Example
almanac	a book published yearly that tells facts about a topic for that year	*Baseball Almanac*
atlas	a book of maps and other information about geography	*Time for Kids World Atlas*
dictionary	a book that tells the meanings of words	*Merriam-Webster's Student Dictionary*
encyclopedia	a book or series with articles on many topics	*Encyclopedia Britannica*
Internet	a collection of resources accessed with a computer	www.gastateparks.org
keywords	words used to search for information	alligators, crocodiles, iguanas
magazine	a publication with pictures and articles that comes out on a certain schedule, such as once a month	*Ranger Rick*
newspaper	a publication that provides current news	*The New York Times*
thesaurus	a book that shows synonyms for words you look up	*Roget's Thesaurus*

99

Research

Most topics are now found on the Internet. To use them, you need to know how to use a computer. If you don't know already, you should get to know how a computer works. Learn about software, memory, disk drives, and so on. You should know how to get online and how to save or print out information that you find.

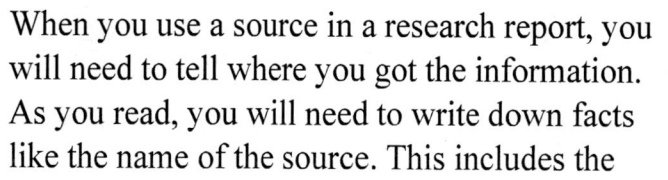

When you use a source in a research report, you will need to tell where you got the information. As you read, you will need to write down facts like the name of the source. This includes the author's name and the date the source was published. What you write down depends on the type of source you use. Your teacher can tell you what facts you should record for each source.

Usually, sources are listed as follows:

Rockwell, Thomas. <u>How to Eat Fried Worms</u>. New York: Yearling, 1973.
    author   title   publisher publisher date
(last name first)   city   name   published

If there is no author, then the title comes first. For Internet sources, you must also list the date when you found the information.

Practice 2: Using Sources

Answer the questions that follow.

1 Which source would be BEST for reading about how your favorite basketball team played yesterday?

    A almanac
    B newspaper
    C encyclopedia
    D atlas

Chapter 7

2 Where would this information MOST LIKELY be found?

- A atlas
- B almanac
- C dictionary
- D thesaurus

3 Which source would be BEST for finding facts about your favorite current singer?

- A dictionary
- B encyclopedia
- C Internet
- D almanac

4 Which source would be BEST for finding a word that means the same thing as *jump*?

- A magazine
- B encyclopedia
- C almanac
- D thesaurus

Research

5 Which source would be BEST for finding the meaning of a word?

- (A) dictionary
- B key word
- C magazine
- D newspaper

6 When you search for information on the Internet, what should you do to get started?

- A Type in keywords.
- (B) Think about your topic.
- C Ask your teacher for help.
- D Tell where you found the facts.

7 Terri is writing a list of the resources she used. Which entry includes all of the needed information?

- (A) Michaels, Peter. <u>Our Species and Our World</u>. Wingate, 2005.
- B Tischler, Tina. <u>Saving the Animals</u>. Chicago: Random House, 2008.
- C Flint, Daniel. <u>Monkeys and Baboons in the Wild</u>. 2007.
- D Payne, Jessica. <u>All the Wild Things.</u> Animal Press Publishers, 2010.

8 If there is not an author's name for an article you find, what should you list first?

- (A) the title of the article
- B the name of the magazine
- C the first word in the article
- D the name of the Web site

Chapter 7

CHAPTER SUMMARY

Books can be divided into parts. Knowing these **organizational features** can help you find what you need.

- A **preface** is a section of a book that gives introductory information.
- A **table of contents** lists the parts of a book in order.
- An **appendix** is extra material at the end of a book.
- A **glossary** is a list of words used in the book.
- An **index** is a list of topics and page numbers at the end of a book.

There are many **types of sources** you can use to find information.

- An **almanac** is a book published yearly that tells about the calendar and weather.
- An **atlas** is a book of maps and other information about geography.
- A **dictionary** is a book that tells the meanings of words.
- An **encyclopedia** is a book or series with articles on many topics.
- The **Internet** is a collection of resources accessed with a computer.
- **Keywords** are words you use to search for information.
- A **magazine** is a booklet published on a certain schedule that has pictures and articles.
- A **newspaper** is a publication that focuses on giving current news.
- A **thesaurus** is a book that shows synonyms for words you look up.

Research

CHAPTER 7 REVIEW

Answer the questions that follow.

1. Where would this information MOST LIKELY be found?

   "Plant corn when the ash-tree leaves are the size of a squirrel's ears."

   - (A) almanac
   - B dictionary
   - C atlas
   - D thesaurus

2. Dom needs to find the definition of a word in a book. Where should he look?

   - A table of contents
   - (B) glossary
   - C index
   - D preface

3. Alice wants to find which pages in her book tell about knitting. Where should she look?

   - A appendix
   - B glossary
   - (C) index
   - D preface

4. Grace is looking for the meaning of the word *patrol*. Where should she look?

   - (A) dictionary
   - B magazine
   - C atlas
   - D almanac

104

Chapter 7

5 **Alejandro is writing a paper about air pollution. Where should he look for facts about the topic?**

    A thesaurus
    B newspaper
    C atlas
    (D) encyclopedia

6 **Jackson's mom is looking for new recipes. Where should she look?**

    (A) cooking magazine
    B encyclopedia
    C atlas
    D dictionary

For questions 7 and 8, use the excerpt from the table of contents below.

Table of Contents

Chapter 1: History of Clocks	page 1
Chapter 2: Kinds of Clocks	page 32
Chapter 3: Unusual Clocks	page 64
Chapter 4: Repairing Clocks	page 80

7 **Which chapter tells how to repair clocks?**

    A Chapter 1
    B Chapter 2
    C Chapter 3
    (D) Chapter 4

8 **Which source listing has all the information needed, in the right order?**

    A Blume, Judy. <u>Superfudge</u>. New York: Puffin, 1980.
    B Judy Blume. <u>Superfudge</u>. Publisher: Puffin, 1980.
    (C) <u>Superfudge</u>. by Judy Blume. New York: Puffin, 1980.
    D Blume, Judy. 1980. <u>Superfudge</u>. Puffin, New York

Research

GA 4 CRCT ELA Practice Test 1

The purpose of this test is to evaluate your skills in a variety of areas linked to the grade 4 English Language Arts standards published by the Georgia Department of Education.

This test is set up in two sections, like the actual CRCT. When you take the CRCT, you have forty-five to seventy minutes to complete each section, with a ten-minute break between them.

GENERAL DIRECTIONS

1 Read all directions carefully.

2 Read each selection.

3 Read each question or example. Then, choose the best answer.

4 Choose only one answer for each question. If you change an answer, be sure to erase the answer completely.

5 At the end of the test, you or your instructor should score your test to see how well prepared you are for the grade 4 CRCT in English Language Arts.

Practice Test 1

Section 1

GA 4 CRCT ELA

1. **The sentence below has a spelling error. Which of the underlined words is spelled incorrectly?**

   Laine <u>mispoke</u> when she shared her <u>view</u> of <u>government</u> during her <u>appearance</u> on the show.

   A mispoke
   B view
   C government
   D appearance

2. **Olivia wrote this note to her science teacher. She wants to revise it to remove anything that does not support her main idea. Which sentence should she remove?**

   ¹ I would like to do a science activity using a hand lens. ² A hand lens helps us see details we might not see with just our eyes. ³ My father gave me a hand lens on my last birthday. ⁴ A hand lens is easy to use and is small enough to fit inside our science kits. ⁵ We could use the tool to study plants, animals, and rocks. ⁶ Learning how to use a hand lens would be a valuable science activity.

   A sentence 2
   B sentence 3
   C sentence 4
   D sentence 5

3. **Look at the underlined word in each sentence. Which sentence uses the underlined word correctly?**

   A After buying the new game, Fred did not have a <u>sent</u> left in his pocket.
   B The teacher <u>scent</u> the three girls to the office to pick up the supplies.
   C Did you receive the letter I <u>cent</u> to you last month?
   D The heavy <u>scent</u> of the roses filled the garden.

109

Practice Test 1

4 **Which type of sentence is this?**

> The sun is shining brightly, but it is still cold outside.

A declarative C interrogative
B imperative D exclamatory

5 **What is the simple predicate of the sentence?**

> Popcorn always tastes much better in a movie theater.

A Popcorn C tastes
B always D in

6 **Which part of speech is the underlined word?**

> The third <u>girl</u> in our row is the tallest person in the room.

A noun C adverb
B verb D adjective

7 **The writer wants to add a sentence to the start of paragraph 2. Which choice would BEST link the paragraphs?**

> Two of the most common kinds of bridges are the beam bridge and the drawbridge. The beam bridge is used to span short distances of no more than 250 feet. It is most often used in roads. This kind of bridge has strong supports along the edges. A long beam is laid over a gap in the road. The gap is caused by water, a ditch, or a lower roadway. Boards, metal, or concrete is laid over the beams and supports. This makes the bridge surface level with the road surface.
>
> Drawbridges are built over bodies of water. A drawbridge has a section in the middle that lifts up. When the section is drawn back, a gap forms in the center of the bridge. Tall ships can pass through the space to get to the other side of the bridge. If a long bridge is needed to span the water, only a part of it will be a drawbridge.

A Like the beam bridge, the drawbridge usually spans a short space.
B Tower Bridge is a famous drawbridge in England.
C Without drawbridges, tall ships could not travel some water routes.
D Have you ever crossed over or through a drawbridge?

GA 4 CRCT ELA

8 Which sentence uses the correct end mark? 4C1c

    A   Nick is the boy who won the race?
    B   The race was held in the afternoon?
    C   It would have been a faster race if it hadn't rained?
    D   Were you at the race last week at the high school?

9 Which is a complete sentence? 4C1c

    A   The musicians in the orchestra.
    B   Everyone in the black-and-white suits.
    C   My sister was playing the piano.
    D   Playing one of my favorite old songs.

10 Which choice correctly breaks the sentence between the subject and the predicate? 4C1a

    A   The big red truck brought / blankets to the camp.
    B   The big red truck / brought blankets to the camp.
    C   The big red truck brought blankets / to the camp.
    D   The big / red truck brought blankets to the camp.

Read the glossary.

> **cyclone** – a storm of spinning winds that moves about 20–30 miles per hour
>
> **hurricane** – a storm with winds moving at least 74 miles per hour, often with thunder, lightning, and heavy rain
>
> **tornado** – a storm of spinning wind with a funnel cloud that travels along a narrow path

11 Which is true of all three weather conditions? 4W3b

    A   They all move at the same speed.
    B   They all are wind storms.
    C   They all include thunder.
    D   They all travel along a narrow path.

Practice Test 1

12 **Which underlined word in the sentence should start with a capital letter?**

> Have you or your sister ever met uncle Dean?

- A you
- B your
- C sister
- (D) uncle

13 **Which sentence uses the correct end mark?**

- A How can I reach your brother!
- B I would like to talk with him?
- (C) Wow, I can't wait to meet him!
- D Did you know he would win.

14 **Which sentence would BEST support the main idea of the paragraph?**

> Students should be allowed to ride their bikes to school for the school day. Riding a bike is excellent exercise, something we all need. The town has recently put new bike paths that lead to the school. We are already allowed to ride bikes for afterschool activities, so everyone knows it is a safe practice. Please, allow us to start riding our bikes to school for the school day.

- (A) The school already owns bike racks.
- B Many students walk to school now.
- C I just got a new bike and helmet for my birthday.
- D Bicycles come in many sizes, colors, and styles.

15 **Which sentence is written correctly?**

- A The boy shoot a basket.
- (B) The boys shoot hoops every day.
- C The girls shoots hoops too.
- D We shoots baskets in the gym.

112

GA 4 CRCT ELA

16 Which is the BEST closing sentence for the paragraph? 4W2Per f

> Every student should take part in Volunteer Week. There are many people in need of help in our community. By helping others, we help ourselves. We learn how to work toward a goal. We learn how to work with others. We also gain respect for others when we understand their needs.

- A This year I am in charge of Volunteer Week.
- B Reading is another good way of spending your time.
- (C) Taking part in Volunteer Week makes us and our community stronger.
- D One popular area is helping with the bike inspections, so you can be outside.

17 Which part of speech is the underlined word? 4C1b

> My father rolled the dough for the pasta.

- A noun
- (B) verb
- C adverb
- D adjective

18 Jon is writing a letter to his parents asking for permission to adopt a dog. Which sentence would BEST support his purpose? 4W2Pers c

- A I read a book about dogs.
- B My friends all have dogs.
- C The neighbor's dog is really friendly and quiet.
- (D) I have always been responsible about my chores.

19 Which word in the sentence needs a period after it? 4C1c

> When did you go to see Dr Gomez at the Doctor's Park building?

- (A) Dr
- B Gomez
- C Park
- D building

Practice Test 1

20 Read the sentences. Which underlined word is spelled incorrectly?

> We went <u>skateing</u> in the park. Catherine kept <u>slipping</u> on the ice. I kept <u>helping</u> her back up. Then, suddenly, it was me <u>falling</u>!

- (A) skateing
- B slipping
- C helping
- D falling

21 Which sentence BEST joins the information in the underlined sentences?

> If someone in Minnesota asks you to meet him by the lake, ask for details. Minnesota is known as the "Land of Ten Thousand Lakes." However, there are actually more than twelve thousand lakes in the state. <u>At least ninety-one of them have the same name. They are named Long Lake.</u> So if your friend wants to meet you at Long Lake, ask for more information.

- A At least ninety-one of them are named Long Lake.
- B At least ninety-one of them have the same name; it is Long Lake.
- (C) Long Lake is the name of ninety-one lakes which have the same name.
- D At least ninety-one have the same name, and it is Long Lake.

22 Which underlined word should start with a capital letter?

> Last <u>weekend</u>, we went to see the <u>picasso</u> exhibit at the <u>museum</u>.

- A weekend
- (B) picasso
- C exhibit
- D museum

114

23 In which sentence is the underlined word used correctly? 4C1g

   A   I <u>past</u> your house today.
   B   Did I meet you in the <u>past</u>?
   C   If I had a real time machine, I would travel to the <u>passed</u>.
   D   My dog's <u>passed</u> owner moved to a no-pets-allowed building.

24 Which sentence is written correctly? 4C1c

   A   My older brother always write the beginning of a story.
   B   My uncle write the ending of the story and sends it back.
   C   My aunt writes to me every week.
   D   I always writes back to my aunt.

25 Which is a complete sentence? 4C1c

   A   The fifteen cows in my neighbor's pasture.
   B   Provide plenty of fresh milk.
   C   Lots of tall grass for munching.
   D   My neighbor uses the milk to make cheese.

26 Where is the BEST place to separate this run-on sentence into two sentences? 4C1c

   | Theresa hopes the bus will come soon she needs to get home. |

   A   after *hopes*
   B   after *bus*
   C   after *soon*
   D   after *needs*

27 Which is a compound sentence? 4C1h

   A   The full moon lit up the dark, crooked trail at night.
   B   I walked down the path, and I stood on the deserted pier.
   C   The soft, glowing moonlight made the water look like glass.
   D   I wished I could have stayed out by the lake a little longer.

Practice Test 1

28 What kind of sentence is below?

> Follow my directions.

- (A) imperative
- B declarative
- C exclamatory
- D interrogative

29 Read the sentence below. Which choice corrects the mistake in the sentence?

> Last year, we went to New York city and saw the Statue of Liberty.

- A Last year, we went to New York city and saw the statue of liberty.
- B Last year, we went to new York city and saw the Statue of Liberty.
- C Last year, we went to New York city and saw the statue of Liberty.
- (D) Last year, we went to New York City and saw the Statue of Liberty.

30 What is the complete subject in the sentence below?

> My sister and my brother are both older than I am.

- A My sister
- B my brother
- (C) My sister and my brother
- D My sister and my brother are both

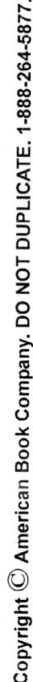

Section 2

Practice Test 1

31 **What kind of sentence is this?**

> Where is the elephant exhibit?

- A imperative
- B declarative
- C exclamatory
- D interrogative

32 **What is the BEST closing sentence for the paragraph?**

> When the teacher called her name, Judy's heart sank in her chest. She did not want to be a judge in the sculpture contest. Judy worried that she would not be fair to everyone, or that she would hurt someone's feelings. She spoke to the teacher about her problem, and the teacher told her not to worry so much.

- A The sculpture of a bear was great.
- B Judy went to the movies later on.
- C She knew Judy would be fair and kind to everyone.
- D There are many times when life does not seem fair.

33 **What part of speech is the underlined word?**

> The <u>slippery</u> eel was too hard to catch.

- A noun
- B verb
- C adverb
- D adjective

34 **Which sentence uses the correct end mark?**

- A Have you ever tried to lead a donkey.
- B A donkey is usually not a good follower.
- C A donkey usually goes wherever it wants to go?
- D It can be a very stubborn animal?

35 What kind of organization does this paragraph use?

> Do you know how fingernails grow? The part of the fingernail we see is called the nail plate. It is made from living cells. The living cells are made under the skin, where we don't see. This part of the fingernail, under the skin, is called the matrix. As the matrix makes new cells, it pushes the old cells upward. The old cells become part of the nail plate. Do fingernails all grow at the same rate? No, they don't! In general, boys' nails grow faster than girls' nails. If you are right-handed, the fingernails on your right hand grow faster than the nails on your left hand. As we get older, our nails grow more slowly.

- A cause and effect
- B chronological order
- C question and answer
- D similarity and difference

36 What is the subject of the sentence?

> My mom's grandfather delivered ice to people's houses.

- A My mom
- B grandfather
- C ice
- D houses

37 Which topic would work BEST for a three-page research paper?

- A Where can you see the Lincoln Memorial?
- B When did Abraham Lincoln become president?
- C When was Abraham Lincoln born?
- D Why is Abraham Lincoln still admired today?

Abraham Lincoln

Practice Test 1

38 Look at the underlined words in the sentence. Which is spelled incorrectly?

> The <u>women</u> tried to sneak past the <u>wolfs</u> <u>unnoticed</u> and run to their <u>cabins</u>.

A women
B wolfs
C unnoticed
D cabins

39 What detail should be added to the paragraph?

> Have you ever tried to take a shortcut through someone else's property? In 1904, the United States got permission from Panama to do just that. At that time, ships that needed to pass from the Atlantic to the Pacific Oceans had to take an eight-thousand-mile trip. They had to go all the way around the tip of South America. The journey was long and dangerous. The shortcut that the United States built is a canal fifty-one miles long. The Panama Canal is a series of lakes and locks. At one end is the Atlantic Ocean, and at the other end is the Pacific Ocean. The two oceans do not have the same sea levels and tides. As ships pass through the canal, they are raised or lowered to stay at sea level. Since it first opened, millions of people have passed through this shortcut.

A Always get permission before cutting through someone else's yard.
B South America is one of the seven continents, or large landmasses.
C The word *lock* has many meanings.
D The canal was completed in 1914.

40 Which sentence uses the underlined word correctly?

A My new puppy kept chasing its own <u>tale</u>.
B Ricky only caught the <u>tale</u> end of the television show.
C The kite <u>tail</u> looked like a snake in the sky.
D That is an old <u>tail</u> that only small children believe.

41 Which part of speech is the underlined word?

> She sewed the button on with <u>silver</u> thread.

A noun
B verb
C adverb
D) adjective

42 What is the BEST closing sentence for the paragraph?

> April Fools' Day is a special celebration of being silly. On April 1, people play harmless tricks on friends and family. The origin of this holiday is unknown. However, records show it has been around for hundreds of years. The custom of playing April Fools' tricks came to America from Great Britain. In the United States, people say, "April fool!" after they play a trick or prank on someone. In France, the person who is tricked is called an April fish. In Scotland, the person is called a gowk or a cuckoo. No matter what term you use, it's important to keep the fun harmless.

A) A joke that leaves everyone smiling is a wonderful way to celebrate the day.
B Not all holidays are silly fun; many holidays celebrate great accomplishments.
C The library has many books of jokes and funny tricks to play on friends.
D April also brings us early spring weather, like rainstorms and warmer days.

43 What is the simple subject of the sentence?

> The young man ran quickly across the stage.

A young
B man
C) quickly
D) stage

Practice Test 1

44 What part of speech is the underlined word? 4C1b

> Peter Pan <u>bravely</u> fought off the pirates.

A noun   B verb   C adverb   D adjective

45 Which sentence uses commas correctly? 4C1c

A The mixture was made up of stones, sand, and concrete.
B The mixture was made up of, stones sand and concrete.
C The mixture was made up of stones, sand, and, concrete.
D The mixture was made up of stones sand, and concrete.

Here is a resource that Leslie used for a report.

> Novak, Lori. <u>Endangered Animals</u>. _____ : Revolutionary Press, 2009.

46 What goes in the blank? 4W3a

A author's last name   C title of the book
B author's first name   D publisher city

47 Which sentence should be added to support the main idea in this paragraph? 4W2Lit c

> The island was the perfect setting for the story. The main problem was that Snap did not feel confident. He was unsure about his ability to lead. There was plenty of food and shelter on the island. In fact, Snap had all he needed to survive the week. However, he had to make decisions about how to use what he had. By the end of the week, Snap had changed from a soldier lost without his leader to a general leading an army of one.

A The island was one of several islands in the lake.
B Alone on the island, Snap had to make every decision.
C Some days, it rained on the island from morning until midnight.
D Unfortunately, there was no pizza, which was Snap's favorite food.

GA 4 CRCT ELA

48 Which sentence should be removed from the paragraph? 4W2Lit e

> ¹ The school in the book is very much like our school. ² In the book, there is a group of popular kids who seem to make all of the decisions. ³ In our school, there is also a group of kids like this. ⁴ In our school, another group of kids hangs out by the swings at recess. ⁵ In the book, there are kind teachers and really tough teachers. ⁶ In our school, we also have a mix of kind and tough teachers.

A sentence 2
B sentence 3
C sentence 4
D sentence 5

49 A student wants to add the following sentence to the paragraph. 4W4b

It also does not lose its vitamin value when being canned.

Where in the paragraph is the BEST place to add the sentence?

> ¹ One of the two types of peaches is the clingstone peach. ² The name comes from the way the fruit clings to its pit or stone. ³ It does not easily pull away from the peach pit. ⁴ Clingstone, or cling, peaches are mainly sold as a canned product. ⁵ The pit is removed and the peaches are halved, sliced, or diced. ⁶ The cling peach is perfect for canning. ⁷ It holds its flavor and texture in the canning process. ⁸ Along with being sweet and juicy, cling peaches are good for you. ⁹ Eating cling peaches helps people fight off colds and other illnesses.

A after sentence 3
B after sentence 5
C after sentence 7
D after sentence 9

50 Duc is looking in the dictionary for the definition of *precious*. He can find this word on the page with what guidewords (starting and ending words) at the top of the page? 4W3c

A pad / palm
B pant / partner
C porter / preparation
D professor / proof

123

Practice Test 1

51 Jorge is reading a book about Samuel "Uncle Sam" Wilson. Look at the book's table of contents below. Where will he find information about where Wilson grew up?

Table of Contents
Childhood 2
Meeting Betsy 9
Leaving New Hampshire 15
Opening a Brick Business 22
Becoming a Meatpacker 30
Marrying Betsy 35
Sharing a Nickname 42

A page 2   B page 9   C page 15   D page 42

52 Which choice is a functional fragment?

A Which one?   C What gladly?
B In starlight.   D Sings nicely.

53 What is the BEST closing sentence for the paragraph?

> The book's conclusion is not satisfying. At least, the readers do learn how the museum statue was stolen, and who stole it. However, there were many subplots in this book. Most of them are never tied up. Readers never learn what happens to Mrs. Pennywhittle. Does she keep her farm, or lose it? The ending also doesn't clear up the relationship between Martha and George. Do they forgive each other and save their friendship?

A I often wonder about the statues I see in museums.
B The main characters did seem like real people though.
C The author should have tied up the loose ends to give the readers a more satisfying finish.
D I think Martha and George should stay friends, so the author can write another book about them.

54 To erase the last letter you just typed, which key would you hit on the keyboard?   4W3d

     A   Escape
     (B)   Backspace
     C   Caps Lock
     D   Page Down

55 A student is writing directions for making a paper airplane. What kind of organization is BEST for the writer to use?   4W1a

     (A)   step order
     B   time order
     C   problem and solution
     D   similarity and difference

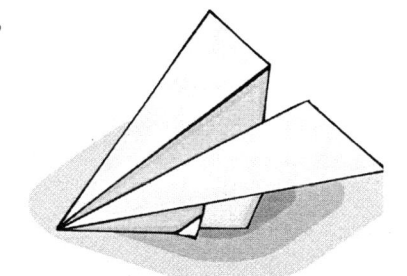

56 How is the paragraph organized?   4W1c

> Mary knew she couldn't take the suitcase with her on the plane if she couldn't close it. She pressed down on the lid of the suitcase, but it bounced back open. So, she tried sitting on the suitcase. Next, she tried holding the lid down with one arm while she tried locking it with the other. Nothing worked. She opened the case and sorted through her belongings. She divided the objects into two piles: "must have" and "can live without." Then, she carefully folded the first pile and placed it neatly back in the suitcase. She closed the suitcase easily. Mary smiled as she realized that she could even fit a few items from the second pile in the suitcase too!

     A   compare and contrast
     B   question and answer
     (C)   problem and solution
     D   cause and effect

57 Which is the complete predicate in the sentence?   4C1a

> The chef mixed three eggs into the batter.

     A   The chef
     B   The chef mixed
     C   chef mixed three eggs
     (D)   mixed three eggs into the batter

Practice Test 1

58 Which sentence uses correct subject-verb agreement? 4C1c

- A The birds build a nest in the tree every year.
- B The groundhog build his home underground.
- C The rabbits builds their dens under the deck.
- D We builds a fence to keep them out of the garden.

59 Look at the underlined sentence. What change BEST improves the flow of the sentences? 4W1d

> Max knew how much his little sister wanted to learn how to ride her bike without training wheels. He knew he needed to be patient. On her first trip down the block, Max held the handlebars with one hand and the back of her seat with his other hand. His sister gripped his hand instead of the handlebars. By the time they reached the corner, Max couldn't feel his fingers. <u>His sister ran over his foot.</u> Max wasn't sure he would survive his sister's lessons.

- A Max could feel it when his sister ran over his foot.
- B It wasn't funny when his sister ran over his foot.
- C On the next trip down the block, his sister ran over his foot.
- D His sister ran over his foot after Max couldn't feel his fingers.

60 Deshaun is writing a letter to a business. He is inviting the owner to visit the school and speak to the students. Which sentence works BEST for this purpose? 4W1a

- A Make sure you answer this letter, since it is a class assignment for me.
- B You should be glad to get the invitation, since we shop at your store.
- C All of the students will appreciate you sharing your knowledge with us.
- D Hey, can you come during fifth period? (I don't like that class!)

GA 4 CRCT ELA Practice Test 2

The purpose of this test is to evaluate your skills in a variety of areas linked to the grade 4 English Language Arts standards published by the Georgia Department of Education.

This test is set up in two sections, like the actual CRCT. When you take the CRCT, you have forty-five to seventy minutes to complete each section, with a ten-minute break between them.

GENERAL DIRECTIONS

1 Read all directions carefully.

2 Read each selection.

3 Read each question or example. Then, choose the best answer.

4 Choose only one answer for each question. If you change an answer, be sure to erase the answer completely.

5 At the end of the test, you or your instructor should score your test to see how well prepared you are for the fourth-grade CRCT in English Language Arts.

Practice Test 2

Section 1

GA 4 CRCT ELA

1. Look at the underlined word in each sentence below. Which sentence uses the underlined word correctly?

    A I live down the <u>rode</u> from the school.
    B I grabbed the oars and <u>rowed</u> to safety.
    C I <u>road</u> my bike to school yesterday.
    D I fell on the <u>rode</u> and cut myself.

2. Which type of sentence is this?

    > The author was signing books at the store.

    A declarative
    B imperative
    C interrogative
    D exclamatory

3. What detail should be added to the following paragraph?

    > The White House is like a work in progress. President George Washington had more to do with the building of the White House than any other president. He helped pick out the place to build the house. For eight years, he oversaw its construction. Yet, Washington never lived inside the White House. President John Adams and his wife were the first to live in the house. Since then, every president, including Adams, made changes to the building. Sometimes, it was made larger. Other times, it was just decorated differently. At times, the changes were based on wants, such as someone's love for the color blue. Other times, the changes were based on needs. Through all of the changes, the outer stone walls remained in place.

    A Many presidents also had summer homes they could visit.
    B Another great place to visit in Washington, D.C., is the National Zoo.
    C There were two major fires, after which many rooms had to be rebuilt.
    D A president is elected every four years, but some serve more than once.

Practice Test 2

4 What is the simple predicate of the following sentence?   4C1a

> The top quickly spun off of the tabletop.

- A quickly
- (B) spun
- C off
- D tabletop

5 Which part of speech is the underlined word below?   4C1b

> The decorated <u>box</u> held a special surprise.

- A verb
- (B) noun
- C adverb
- D adjective

6 Bruce is writing a list of the resources he used for his report. Which entry includes all of the needed information?   4W3a

- A Newton, Joel. <u>Energy</u>. Sacramento: California Press.
- B France, Gary David. <u>Clean Energy</u>. New York, 2005.
- (C) Walker, Judy. <u>Wind Power</u>. Chicago: Science Press, 2010.
- D Costi, Margaret. <u>Renewable Energy</u>. American Publishing.

7 Which sentence below uses the correct end mark?   4C1c

- A How much does the market charge for a pear.
- B Can you choose between several kinds of pears.
- (C) Have you ever purchased a pear there?
- D The store clerk is always nice to everyone?

130

GA 4 CRCT ELA

8 What is the BEST closing sentence for this paragraph? 4W2Info h

> Karel Appel was an artist who liked finding new ways to express himself. In 1947, he developed a new style of art. Appel would build a kind of relief collage. He would use wood and found objects in his pieces. About nine years later, Appel decided to try something new. He began working with stained glass. Over the next few years, he built murals and windows out of the glass. His passion for new ideas led him to experiment successfully with cloth, marble, ceramics, and concrete. He continued to build relief pieces and added painting to his works.

A By using many different materials, Karel Appel was always able to find new ways to share his ideas.

B Stained glass was not a new idea; many other artists used this material for centuries before Appel.

C There was a large group of experimental artists living in Denmark at the time.

D Many artists will use the same materials, but learn to use those materials in new ways.

9 Which is a complete sentence? 4C1c

A Thunder, lightning, and strong winds.

B Shook the house and the windows.

C After the storm, bright sunny skies.

D It was a perfect day to be outside.

10 Which choice correctly breaks the sentence between the subject and the predicate? 4C1a

A My youngest / brother is an excellent math student.

B My youngest brother is an excellent / math student.

C My youngest brother / is an excellent math student.

D My / youngest brother is an excellent math student.

Practice Test 2

11 Look at the underlined words in the sentence below. Which is spelled incorrectly?

> The <u>people</u> were <u>joyfully</u> <u>celebrating</u> the <u>holidayes</u>.

A people
B joyfully
C celebrating
D holidayes

12 Which is the BEST closing sentence for this paragraph?

> Our school should change to a four-day school week. Many places have already made this change and found many benefits. For example, the schools found that attendance improved. It also saved the schools money. A four-day school week means you don't have to heat or light the buildings on Fridays. You also don't have to run school buses on Fridays. Plus, the teachers say that the students get used to the longer school day quickly.

A Some schools encourage students to join a team or band.
B The switch to a four-day school week would be a positive change.
C Students won't need to take days off to make dentist appointments.
D There are many new ideas in the world, and all of them are worth trying.

13 Which sentence below uses the underlined word correctly?

A Can you <u>hear</u> the children singing?
B My cousin moved <u>hear</u> from Texas.
C Can you come when you <u>here</u> me call?
D I never did <u>here</u> what grade he got.

GA 4 CRCT ELA

14 Which sentence would support the following idea?

> The maps in the book were a great addition.

- A The author should have included more illustrations.
- B Seeing the maps of the area made it easier to picture how it would look.
- C I think, however, that the ending of the book was much too hard to believe.
- D I never use maps to find locations that I need to visit.

15 Elena is reading a book about Woodrow Wilson. Where in the book will she find information about when Wilson became president?

Table of Contents
Early Life 2
College 9
Governor Wilson 15
President Wilson 22
War 30
League of Nations 35
After the White House 42

- A page 9
- B page 15
- C page 22
- D page 42

16 Which part of speech is the underlined word?

> Her baby sister cries <u>loudly</u> at night.

- A verb
- B noun
- C adverb
- D adjective

17 Where is a period needed in the sentence below?

> Did Mrs White work in the dentist's office on Park Street?

- A after Mrs
- B after White
- C after dentist's
- D after Street

133

Practice Test 2

18 Which of the following is a complete sentence? 4C1c

  A A picnic basket for sandwiches.
  B I brought some sliced fruit to eat.
  C A large pitcher of lemonade.
  D Found a clean picnic table nearby.

19 What is the BEST place to separate this run-on sentence into two sentences? 4C1c

| Stephen scored the winning goal the excited crowd cheered loudly. |

  A after *scored*
  B after *goal*
  C after *crowd*
  D after *cheered*

20 What is the BEST closing sentence for this paragraph? 4W2Lit f

| My favorite character in the book is Jin because he reminds me of my best friend, Mark. Jin is smart. He always knows where to go to get the information he needs. He is not afraid to take chances or to try new things. He is always there for his best friend, Lou, even when Lou finds himself in a real pinch. All of these things also describe Mark. |

  A Since Mark is my best friend, it makes sense that Jin would be my favorite character.
  B I also loved the setting, because I would love to be locked inside an amusement park!
  C I read at least one book a month, so I know what a good book looks like.
  D The title of the book did not give any hint for what the story was about.

21 Which of the following is a compound sentence? 4C1h

  A A honeybee flew from flower to flower.
  B A robin brought a worm to its babies.
  C Playing outside all day, the children were happy.
  D Andrew threw the ball, and Joel caught the ball.

134

GA 4 CRCT ELA

22 What kind of sentence is this? 4C1h

Answer the door.

A   imperative
B   declarative
C   exclamatory
D   interrogative

23 Read the sentence below. Which choice corrects the mistake in the sentence? 4C1c

I saw Mrs. Ryan at Green middle School on Monday afternoon.

A   I saw Mrs. Ryan at green middle school on Monday afternoon.
B   I saw Mrs. Ryan at Green Middle school on Monday afternoon.
C   I saw Mrs. Ryan at Green Middle School on monday afternoon.
D   I saw Mrs. Ryan at Green Middle School on Monday afternoon.

24 What is the complete subject in the sentence below? 4C1a

A beautiful mix of flowers grows in my garden.

A   flowers
B   mix of flowers
C   A beautiful mix of flowers
D   A beautiful mix of flowers grows

25 Which of these choices is a functional fragment? 4C1h

A   Snowy.
B   Soup.
C   Through?
D   Yummy!

26 Which is the complete predicate in the following sentence? 4C1a

Janet and Chris ran in the marathon last month.

A   Janet and Chris
B   Janet and Chris ran
C   ran in the marathon
D   ran in the marathon last month

135

Practice Test 2

27 The writer wants to add a sentence to the start of paragraph 2. 4W1d
Which choice would BEST link these paragraphs?

> Kara and Sammy decided to work together to clean the basement. They sorted through the cartons and carried the junk outside. Then they put the remaining items together, grouping things by their use. Finally, they labeled each carton and placed the cartons on a shelf.
>
> They rode their bikes by the fountains and down toward the soccer fields. When they reached the fields, they saw a group of their friends playing. They locked their bikes to the bike rack and joined in the game.

- A When their work was done, they decided to go to the park.
- B They rode their bikes to the park because it was a nice day.
- C Both Kara and Sammy like to ride bikes.
- D There are many things to do at the park.

28 Which sentence uses the correct subject-verb agreement? 4C1c

- A Can Jack digs into his pocket for change?
- B The moles digs holes in the backyard.
- C The children dig in the sandbox.
- D My mother dig in the garden.

29 What part of speech is the underlined word? 4C1b

> The <u>icy</u> wind warned us a winter storm was near.

- A noun
- B verb
- C adverb
- D adjective

30 Which sentence below uses the correct end mark? 4C1c

- A The traffic in the city can be very noisy?
- B The movie was so boring I fell asleep?
- C I wonder who invented the rubber band.
- D Can I go to the library with Danny today.

Section 2

Practice Test 2

31 Which choice correctly places a break between the subject and the predicate?

   A I named my new cat Snowball / because it has white fur.

   B I / named my new cat Snowball because it has white fur.

   C I named / my new cat Snowball because it has white fur.

   D I named my new cat Snowball because it has / white fur.

32 Which topic would work BEST for a one-page essay?

   A the history of the United States

   B the American Revolutionary War

   C the view from a Mississippi River boat

   D the history and geography of Georgia

33 What is the simple subject of the sentence below?

> Harry tossed the pizza dough into the air.

   A Harry   C dough

   B pizza   D air

34 Which sentence should be removed from this paragraph?

> [1] I think *Grains of Sand* was very much like *A Patch of Sun*. [2] Both books had strong main characters who faced similar problems. [3] In *Grains of Sand*, Elizabeth had to find the courage to think for herself and do the right thing—be kind to Ann. [4] In *A Patch of Sun*, Jeremy's friends find a way to sneak into the local movie theater without paying. [5] The movie theater only showed one movie at a time. [6] In the end, Jeremy decides he has to do what he knows is right, no matter what his friends think.

   A sentence 2

   B sentence 3

   C sentence 4

   D sentence 5

GA 4 CRCT ELA

35 What part of speech is the underlined word?

> The snake slithered <u>silently</u> through the sand.

- A noun
- B verb
- **C adverb**
- D adjective

36 Which sentence uses commas correctly?

- A John, Paul, George and, Ringo were members of the Beatles.
- B John, Paul, George and Ringo were members, of the Beatles.
- C John, Paul, George and Ringo, were members of the Beatles.
- **D John, Paul, George, and Ringo were members of the Beatles.**

37 The sentence below has a spelling error. Which of the underlined words is spelled incorrectly?

> I <u>overheared</u> the <u>principal</u> talking about <u>trophies</u> for spelling bee <u>winners</u>.

- **A overheared**
- B principal
- C trophies
- D winners

38 What kind of organization does this paragraph use?

> How does the Arctic fox survive on the frozen tundra it calls home? The animal has many adaptations that help it live. First, it has a thick, white coat. The fur not only helps keep the fox warm, it also helps the fox blend in with the snow. This makes it harder for enemies to find the fox. The fur even covers the soles of its paws. The arctic fox also has a thick, furry tail, which it can use as a blanket on cold, snowy nights.

- A cause and effect
- B chronological order
- **C question and answer**
- D similarity and difference

Practice Test 2

39 What kind of sentence is this?   4C1h

> Can you help me carry this box?

- A   imperative
- B   declarative
- C   exclamatory
- **(D)**   interrogative

40 Which of the sentences below is the BEST closing sentence for this paragraph?   4W2Nar h

> A warm, sunny day makes me feel like Mother Nature is ordering me to go to the beach. I love walking along the wooden planks of the boardwalk. I love listening to the waves kiss the shore. The salty smell of the ocean practically makes me dance. However, I do not like the gulls swooping down by my head. They are like feathered bandits trying to steal some lunch.

- A   Another great way to spend a sunny afternoon is to go hiking in the mountains.
- B   However, this one downfall does not keep me from the beach on a sunny day.
- C   Did you know that the five oceans are all connected?
- D   I do, however, like to go bird watching in the fields.

41 Read the sentences below. Which underlined word is spelled incorrectly?   4C1f, 4W4c

> I love <u>raking</u> leaves. The colors are so <u>pritty</u> in the fall. I even love the <u>noises</u> the leaves make under my rake. They snap and crunch as my rake <u>passes</u> over them.

- A   raking
- **(B)**   pritty
- C   noises
- D   passes

140

42 Which sentence is written correctly? 4C1c

- (A) Taffy sticks to my teeth.
- B Dust and dirt sticks to the paint.
- C Ann and Mark sticks together.
- D Bubbles sticks to the tiles.

43 Which sentence would BEST support the main idea of this paragraph? 4W2Per c

> Our class project should be painting a mural at the senior center. In the past, classes have planted flowers, baked cookies, and hosted tea parties for the center. These were good ideas, but they don't last. A mural will be there for many years. It will make people feel welcome when they enter the building. On Monday, please vote for the mural to be our class project.

- (A) The mural will remind people every day that we appreciate them.
- B Art is my strongest subject, so I could be in charge of the project.
- C I once saw a mural in an office building.
- D The senior center also offers art classes.

44 Which underlined word below should start with a capital letter? 4C1c

> I went to <u>mount</u> Rushmore on vacation last <u>summer</u> with my <u>aunt</u> and <u>uncle</u>.

- (A) mount
- B summer
- C aunt
- D uncle

Practice Test 2

45 A student wants to add the following sentence to the paragraph.

I named him Freckles.

Where in the paragraph does this sentence belong?

> ¹ Mr. Johnson had warned me not to name the puppies that came into the shelter. ² He said it would only make it harder for me when the pups left. ³ I really didn't understand this at first. ⁴ It made me happy to see the dogs find homes with loving families. ⁵ However, I soon came to see the wisdom in Mr. Johnson's words. ⁶ One day, a very playful white pup with black spots came into the shelter. ⁷ When the pup left, it felt like I was giving away my own pet.

- A after sentence 4
- B after sentence 5
- C after sentence 6
- D after sentence 7

46 Where would Carol look for the definition of *droop*?

- A index
- B newspaper
- C almanac
- D dictionary

47 Which of the following is an example of computer hardware?

- A a desk
- B a mouse
- C a game CD
- D a search engine

48 A student is writing an essay about what dolphins and porpoises have in common, and what sets them apart. What kind of organization should the writer use?

- A step order
- B time order
- C problem and solution
- D similarity and difference

GA 4 CRCT ELA

49 How is the following paragraph organized? 4W1c

> A series of storms hit the coast in April. They left behind eroded beaches. The loss of beachfront could greatly affect the area. The animals that live in the sand will need to find new homes. People's homes are in danger too. Those close to the beach are in greater danger of flooding at high tide. In addition, the area could lose business. Fewer visitors will come to visit the beaches. This means fewer people in the shops and restaurants.

A) cause and effect
B question and answer
C problem and solution
D similarity and difference

50 Which sentence uses the correct end mark? 4C1c

A) Watch out!
B That ball is blue!
C Did you see it.
D It belongs to Sam?

51 Look at the paragraph below. What change to the underlined sentence would BEST improve the flow of the paragraph? 4W1d

> Tyler wiped the sweat from his forehead. It had been chilly when he started raking the leaves, but now the hot sun was beating down on him. He was glad to be almost finished with the task. There were six neat mounds of leaves in the yard. In a few minutes, he would be ready to bag all of the piles. Suddenly, a dark cloud rolled overhead, and a strong wind blew. <u>The entire day's work was undone.</u> The leaves were scattered in every direction.

A The entire day's work was undone very quickly.
B After raking, the entire day's work was undone.
C With one gust of wind, the entire day's work was undone.
D It made Tyler angry that the entire day's work was undone.

Practice Test 2

52 Which part of speech is the underlined word below?

> The batter <u>slid</u> into first base.

A   verb
B   noun
C   adverb
D   adjective

53 Emma is writing a letter to her grandmother asking her to come for a visit. Which sentence would BEST support her purpose?

A   Last weekend, I went roller skating at the rink with my friends.
B   I have a new jigsaw puzzle that I think you would love to work on.
C   My best friend's grandmother baked cookies for us yesterday.
D   You live so far away that it will take you a long time to get here.

54 Which sentence BEST joins the information in the underlined sentences?

> The main difference betweens creeks and brooks and rivers is size. <u>Creeks are smaller than rivers. Brooks are smaller than rivers too.</u> They flow downhill and often pour into a river. Because of their small size, creeks and brooks are more likely to dry up without rain than rivers.

A   Both creeks and brooks are smaller than rivers.
B   Creeks and brooks—they're smaller than rivers.
C   Rivers are bigger than both creeks and brooks get.
D   Creeks are smaller than rivers, and brooks are too.

GA 4 CRCT ELA

Read the glossary, then answer the question which follows.

> **frog** – adult stage with smooth, wet skin, strong hind legs, and webbed feet
>
> **froglet** – stage 3 of a frog's development; looks like a frog with a short tail
>
> **spawn** – stage 1 in a frog's development; a group of fertilized frog eggs in a jelly-like covering
>
> **tadpole** – stage 2 of a frog's development; the body has gills and a long tail; the legs develop later

55 Michelle sees a picture of a frog with a long tail and no legs. What stage is she looking at?

    A   adult
    B   froglet
    C   spawn
    D   tadpole

56 Which underlined word in the following sentence should start with a capital letter?

> The <u>store</u> is on Market <u>street,</u> right behind <u>the</u> Museum <u>of</u> Modern Art.

    A   store
    B   street
    C   the
    D   of

57 A student is writing a speech. He wants to convince his fellow students to attend a meeting about homework. Which sentence works BEST for this purpose?

    A   Together, we can make sure our opinions are heard.
    B   The teachers are the experts when it comes to homework.
    C   Actually, I have no idea how to solve this problem.
    D   Parents will have an easier time convincing the board.

Practice Test 2

58 In which sentence below is the underlined word used correctly?

   A   I kept one of the boxes <u>plain</u> and painted the other one.
   B   Latonya realized that the <u>plain was about to take off</u>.
   C   There is a large, flat <u>plane</u> before you get to the mountain.
   D   Joe thinks the food at the new cafe tastes rather <u>plane</u>.

59 Which sentence below is written correctly?

   A   The students practices playing new songs.
   B   Matt and Mike practices playing their drums.
   C   Liz practices playing the viola every day.
   D   The musicians practices music together too.

60 Lila wrote a short story. She wants to revise this paragraph. She wants to move the underlined sentence. Where does the sentence fit BEST in the paragraph?

> [1] Anton and his father climbed up the steep hill just as the sun was setting. [2] When they reached the top, they set up a powerful telescope. [3] Anton's father spread a map of the stars on the ground. [4] Anton studied the map and chose a few stars to search for in the sky. [5] Anton's father showed him how to adjust the telescope. [6] When darkness blanketed the hill, Anton looked through it. [7] The stars looked much bigger and clearer through the lens. [8] Anton soon found the stars he had chosen. <u>Anton's father had given Anton the telescope for his birthday</u>.

   A   after sentence 2
   B   after sentence 3
   C   after sentence 4
   D   after sentence 6

A
abbreviation 40
adjective 27, 29
adverb 27, 29
almanac 99, 103
appendix 96, 103
atlas 99, 103

B
bullet 71

C
capitalization 42, 43, 44
cause and effect paragraph 65, 74
character 81
chronological order 64
chronological paragraph 65, 74
closing sentence 61, 74
comma 41, 44
common noun 24
compare and contrast 65
complete predicate 48
complete subject 48
compound sentence 51, 56
concluding sentence 82
contrasting idea 70

D
declarative sentence 52, 56
detail 85, 86
dictionary 99, 103
drafting 81, 82, 92

E
editing 89, 92
encyclopedia 99, 103
end mark 39, 40, 44
entence fragment 56
exclamation point 39, 44
exclamatory sentence 52, 56

F
focus on writing 82
fragment 54
functional fragment 54, 56

G
glossary 97, 103

H
homophone 34, 36

I
imperative sentence 52, 56
index 97, 103
informational writing 79, 82, 92
Internet 99, 100, 103
interrogative sentence 52, 56
irregular noun 32, 36
irregular verb 26, 33, 36

K
keyword 99, 103

M
magazine 99, 103

main idea 60, 85
mechanics 39

N
narrative writing 79, 82, 92
newspaper 99, 103
noun 23, 24, 29, 31, 32, 36, 49

O
organizational features 95, 103
organizational pattern 64
outline 70, 71

P
paragraph 59, 65, 66, 69, 70, 71, 81, 82, 85
paragraph content 60
paragraph structure 60, 64
paragraph topic 60, 74
parts of speech 23, 29
period 40, 44
persuasive writing 79, 82, 92
plural 31, 32
plural subject 49
plural verb 49
predicate 48, 56
preface 95, 103
prewriting 80, 81, 92
proper adjective 44
proper noun 23, 44
publishing 90, 92
punctuation 39, 40, 89

Q
question and answer paragraph 66, 74
question mark 39, 44

R
regular noun 31, 36
regular verb 25, 32, 36
research 100
response to literature 79, 82, 92
revising 85, 92

S
sentence 47, 56, 59, 61, 69, 70
sentence fragment 54
sentence structure 51
sentence types 52
similarity and difference paragraph 65, 74
simple predicate 48
simple sentence 51, 56
simple subject 48
singular 32
singular subject 49
singular verb 49
source (of information) 95, 99, 103
spelling 89
spelling rule 31, 32, 33, 36
subheading 70, 71
subject 47, 48, 56
subject-verb agreement 49, 56
supporting detail 82, 86
supporting sentence 61, 74, 85
synonym 99, 103

T
table of contents 96, 103

thesaurus 99, 103
topic sentence 61, 74, 82
transirion 74
transition 64, 65, 66, 71, 85, 87
transitional structure 70
transitions between paragraphs 69
type of writing 79, 82

V

verb 25, 29, 32, 33, 36, 47
verb tense 25, 26

W

writing 79, 80
writing process 80, 85, 89, 90, 92